海野勝珉 下絵・資料集
東京芸術大学大学美術館所蔵

UNNO SHOMIN

SKETCHES OF UNNO SHOMIN
—WITHIN THE COLLECTION OF THE UNIVERSITY ART MUSEUM, TOKYO NATIONAL UNIVERSITY OF FINE ARTS AND MUSIC

東方出版

序

海野勝珉（一八四四―一九一五）は明治時代の彫金を代表する存在であり、また東京芸術大学の前身である東京美術学校の創設期から二十世紀初頭までの教授をつとめ、金工家の教育育成に多大な功績を残しました。

九歳より水戸金工家の初代海野美盛と萩谷勝平に彫金を学んだ後に東京で開業したが、明治九（一八七六）年の廃刀令により装剣金具の制作は断念せざるをえませんでした。他の彫金家と同様に新たな時代とニーズに合う花瓶、置物、煙草入や装身具などの作品の制作にうつり、代表作の《蘭陵王置物》（宮内庁三の丸尚蔵館）などの作品を展覧会に出品して、その力量を認められました。明治二十三年に初代東京美術学校彫金科教授の加納夏雄と師弟関係を結び、ともに東京美術学校の金工教育の基礎づくりに尽力しました。また二十九年から帝室技芸員として金工界を先導し、とくに刀装具で培った各種の金属の色を象嵌で表現した彫金を得意としました。

東京芸術大学大学美術館のコレクションには海野勝珉の遺族より昭和四十五（一九七〇）年に寄贈された周辺の作家の作品を含む刀装具から花瓶までの多数の下絵、拓本などの関連資料が保管されています。現存する海野作品の研究材料だけでなく、この時代の彫金研究にも重要な参考資料であるため、大学美術館所蔵資料の活用と研究の一環としてこれを公刊できることは意義深いことといえましょう。これらの研究に貢献できることを期待しつつ、ここにご協力いただきました方々に厚く御礼申しあげます。

東京藝術大学大学美術館

※本頁の作品(手板)のサイズは原寸とは異なる

3	序	Foreword
7	花瓶図案	Flower Vase Designs
39	種々図案	Various Designs
105	手板・煙草入	Metalwork Plates & Cigarette Case
121	拓本	Rubbings
137	海野勝珉関係資料について 横溝廣子	
I		Foreword
II		Reference Materials of Unno Shomin Hiroko Yokomizo

目次 Contents

凡例

1 「花瓶図案」、「種々図案」、「拓本」に掲載されている図版は、東京藝術大学大学美術館所蔵の「海野家資料」(登録番号金工1597)」を撮影したものより抜粋し、編集した。

2 「手板・煙草入」は東京藝術大学大学美術館所蔵品のうち、海野勝珉作の作品を掲載し、登録番号は写真キャプションの最後に示す。

3 「拓本」は、海野勝珉の作品の拓本の一部を選択して掲載した。ただし、122、123ページの拓本は小場恒吉案、清水南山および海野清の構成による法隆寺夢殿救世観音厨子金具の拓本である。

Notes

1 "FLOWER VASE DESIGNS", "VARIOUS DESIGNS", and "RUBBINGS" are selected from the Unno Family Material in the collection of The University Art Museum, Tokyo National University of Fine Arts and Music (Inventory number - Metal 1597)

2 "METALWORK PLATES & CIGARETTE CASE" illustrates the works by Unno Shomin in the collection of The University Art Museum, Tokyo National University of Fine Arts and Music (Inventory number is shown in the last line of the photograph captions).

3 "RUBBINGS" were selected from rubbings of UNNO Shomin's works. However, the rubbings on p.122 and p.123 are rubbings of the metal fittings attached to the shrine for the Kuze Kannon in the Yumedono Hall at Horyuji Temple, designed by OBA Tsunekichi and formed by SHIMIZU Nanzan and UNNO Kiyoshi.

花瓶図案

海野勝珉は、江戸時代の刀装具の制作で培った彫金の技術を新しい時代にふさわしい作品に応用することで明治時代を代表する彫金家として活躍した。その新しい作品の主要なウェイトを占めたのが花瓶であった。東京芸術大学大学美術館所蔵の「海野家資料」に含まれる図案の中で、この花瓶類がまとまって完成度が高く、宮内省などの依頼により数多く制作されたとみなされる。

FLOWER VASE DESIGNS

Unno Shomin was a metal carving artist representative of the Meiji era, applying his techniques to create sword fittings of the Edo period to new forms fit for the new era. One of the major forms was the flower vase. Among the sketches within the Unno Family Material in the collection of The University Art Museum, Tokyo National University of Fine Arts and Music, the design sketches for flower vases are the most complete as a group, and many vases were created according to commissions from the Imperial Household Ministry, and others.

花瓶図案 | Flower Vase Designs

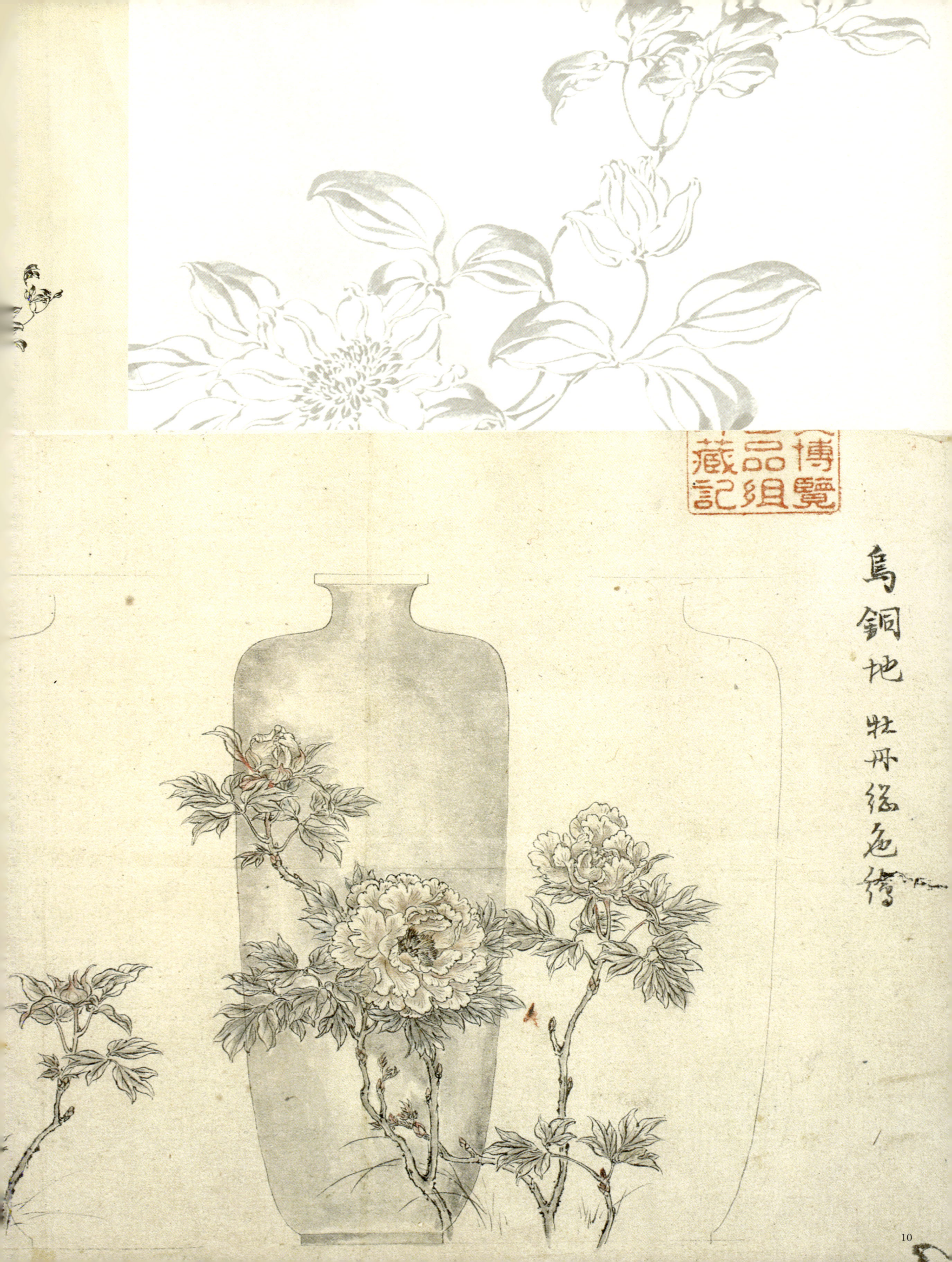

烏銅地牡丹絡危瓶

花瓶図案 | FLOWER VASE DESIGNS

花瓶図案 | Flower Vase Designs

茶蘼 梅花
茉莉 芍藥
梔子

名花十友之圖
菊花　海棠
蓮　　瑞香
巖桂

花瓶図案 | FLOWER VASE DESIGNS

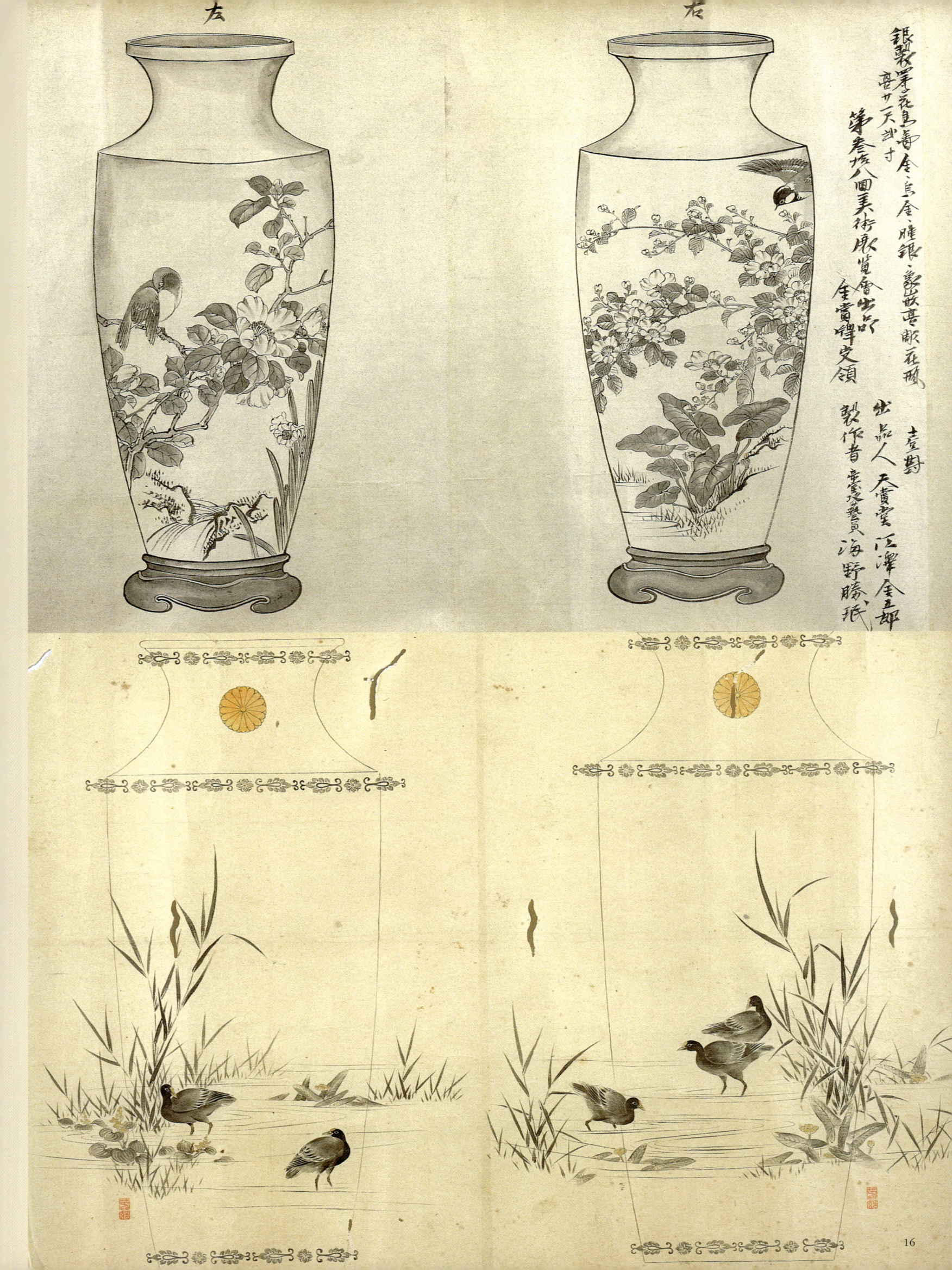

花瓶図案 | FLOWER VASE DESIGNS

純色地 立木鶉色高眼
鷲 四分一

茶真錦地 柏苔少シ菱真錦
フクロ金色修

花瓶図案 | Flower Vase Designs

花瓶図案

Flower Vase Designs

花瓶図案 | Flower Vase Designs

花瓶図案 | FLOWER VASE DESIGNS

花瓶図案 | Flower Vase Designs

花瓶図案 | Flower Vase Designs

花瓶図案 | Flower Vase Designs

31

花瓶図案

Flower Vase Designs

花瓶図案 | Flower Vase Designs

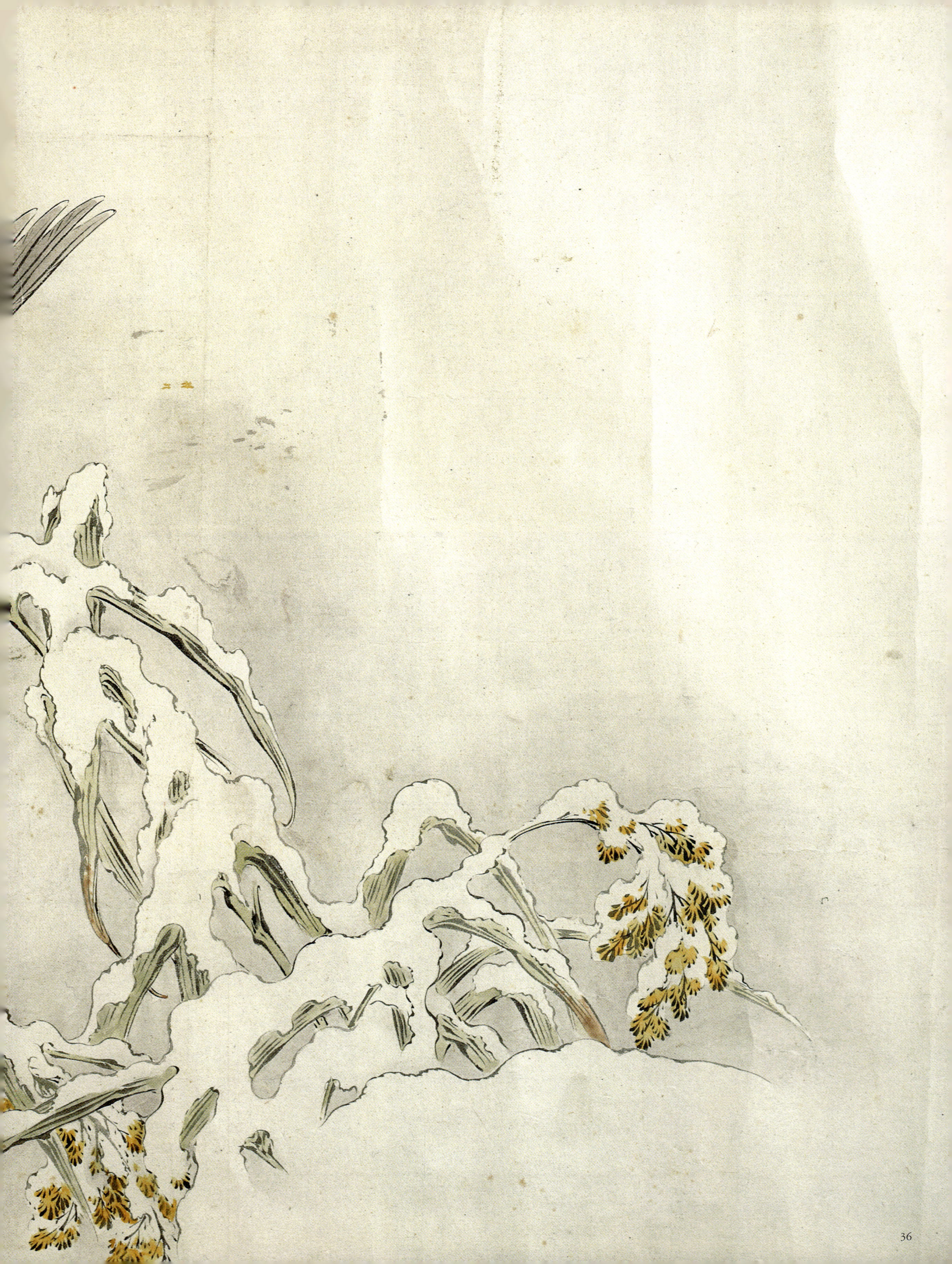

花瓶図案｜Flower Vase Designs

38

種々図案

「海野家資料」には箱、額、煙草入、皿、釦、装身具、置物など、多種多様な図案が描かれている。鍔などの刀装具の図案やその流れを汲んだ豊かな表情の人物や動物もあれば、伝統的な花鳥画や風景画を応用した図案がある。海野勝珉は他の彫金家と違っていずれのモチーフもこなすという定評があった。

VARIOUS DESIGNS

The designs of the Unno family include a wide variety of designs for boxes, framed works, cigarette cases, dishes, buttons, accessories and figurines, etc. There are human and animal figures full of expression, many descended from the styles of sword fittings, and there are designs taken from traditional flower and bird paintings or landscapes. Unno Shomin was known to be superior in either motif, rare among metal carving artists.

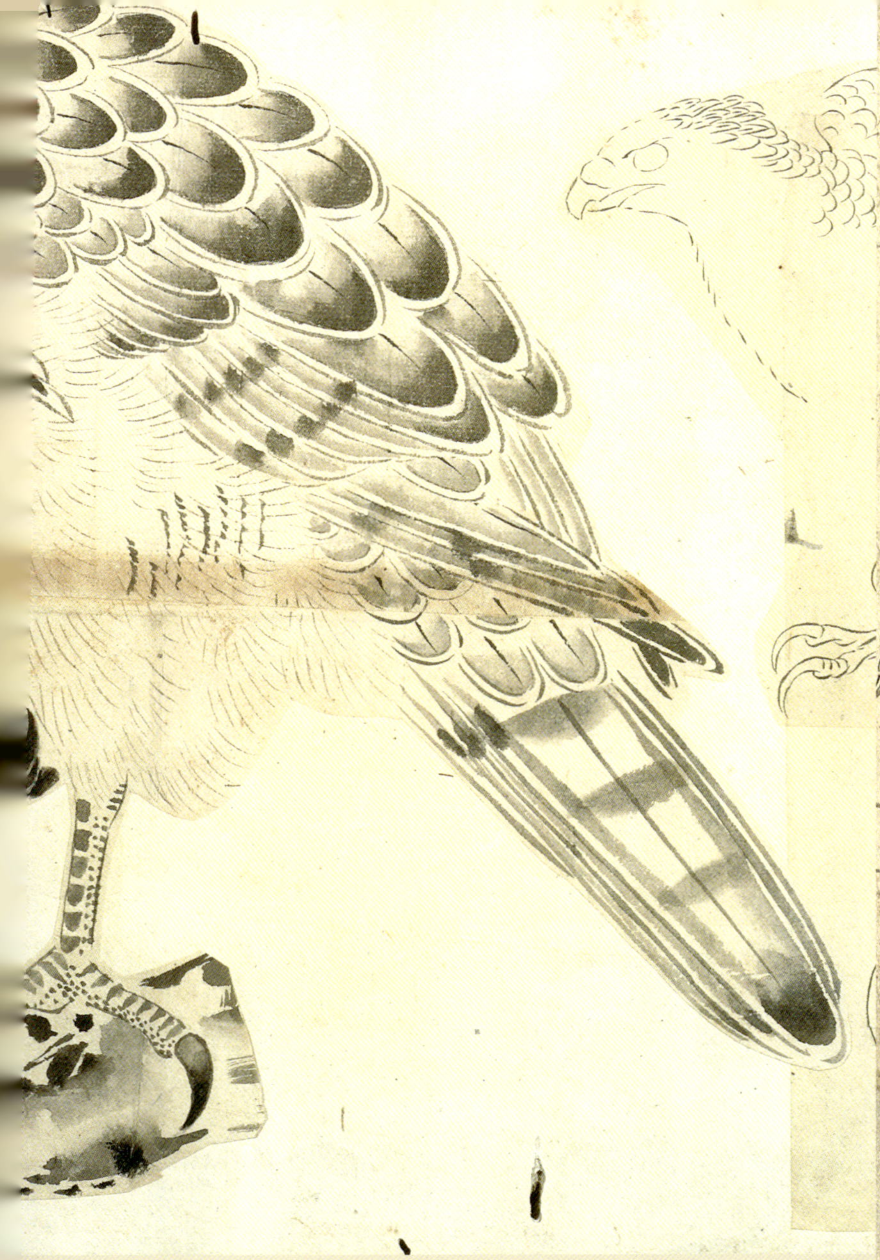

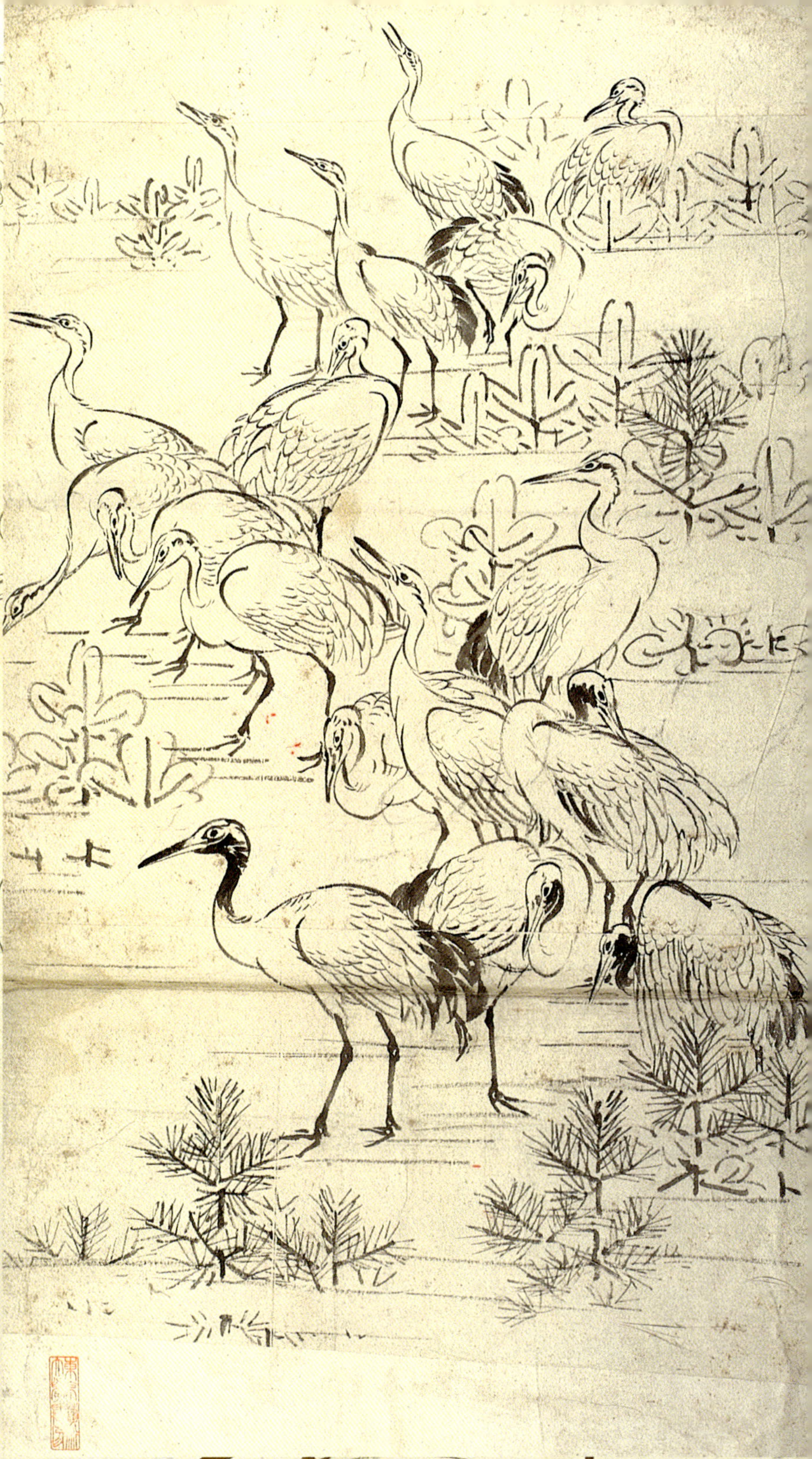

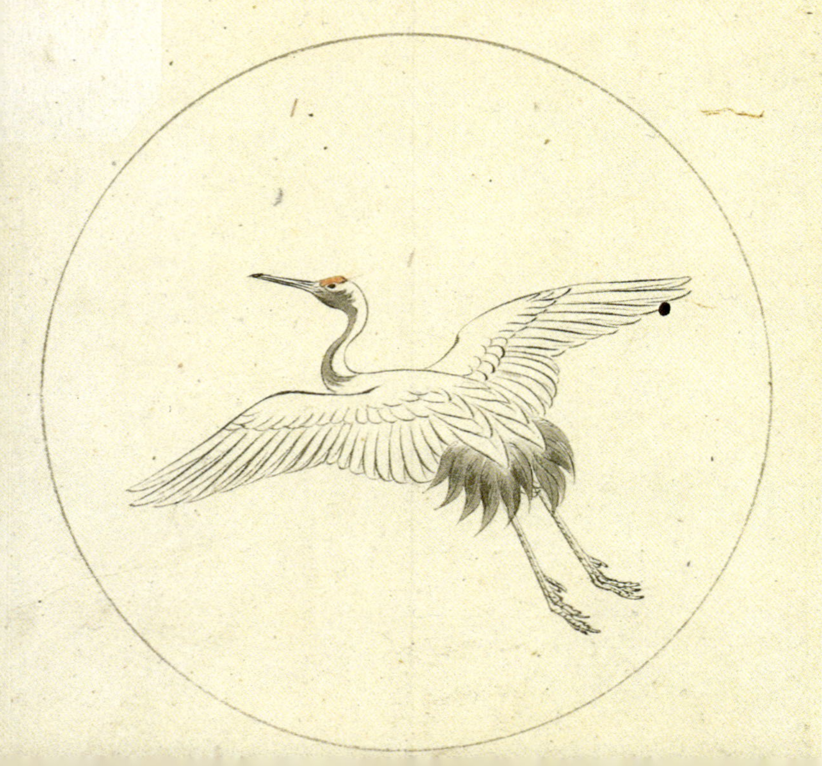

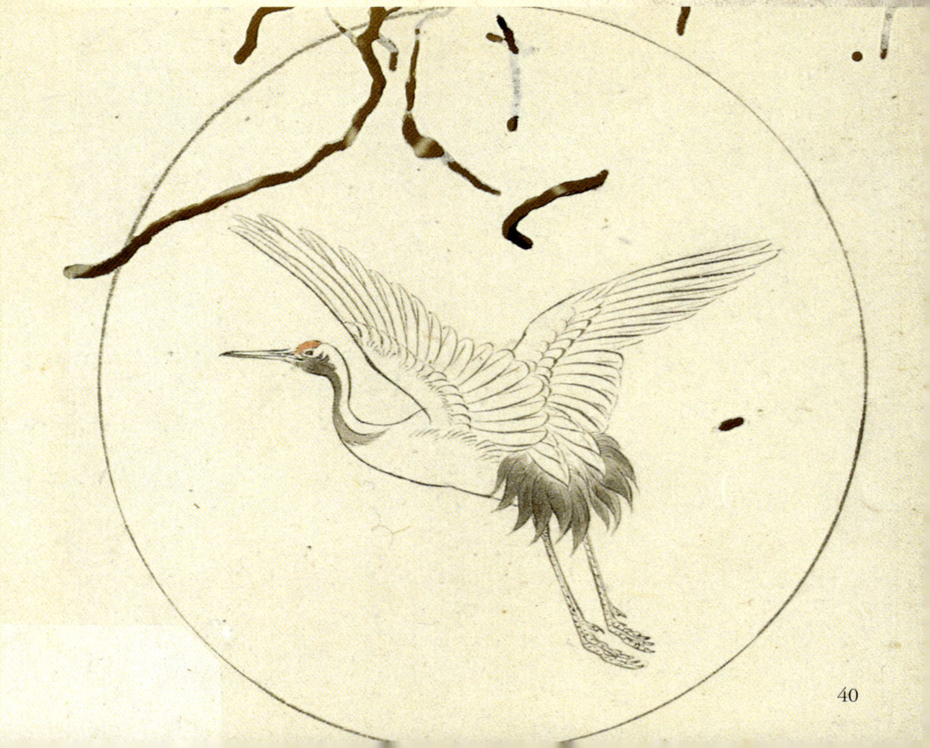

種々図案 | Various Designs

42

種々図案 | Various Designs

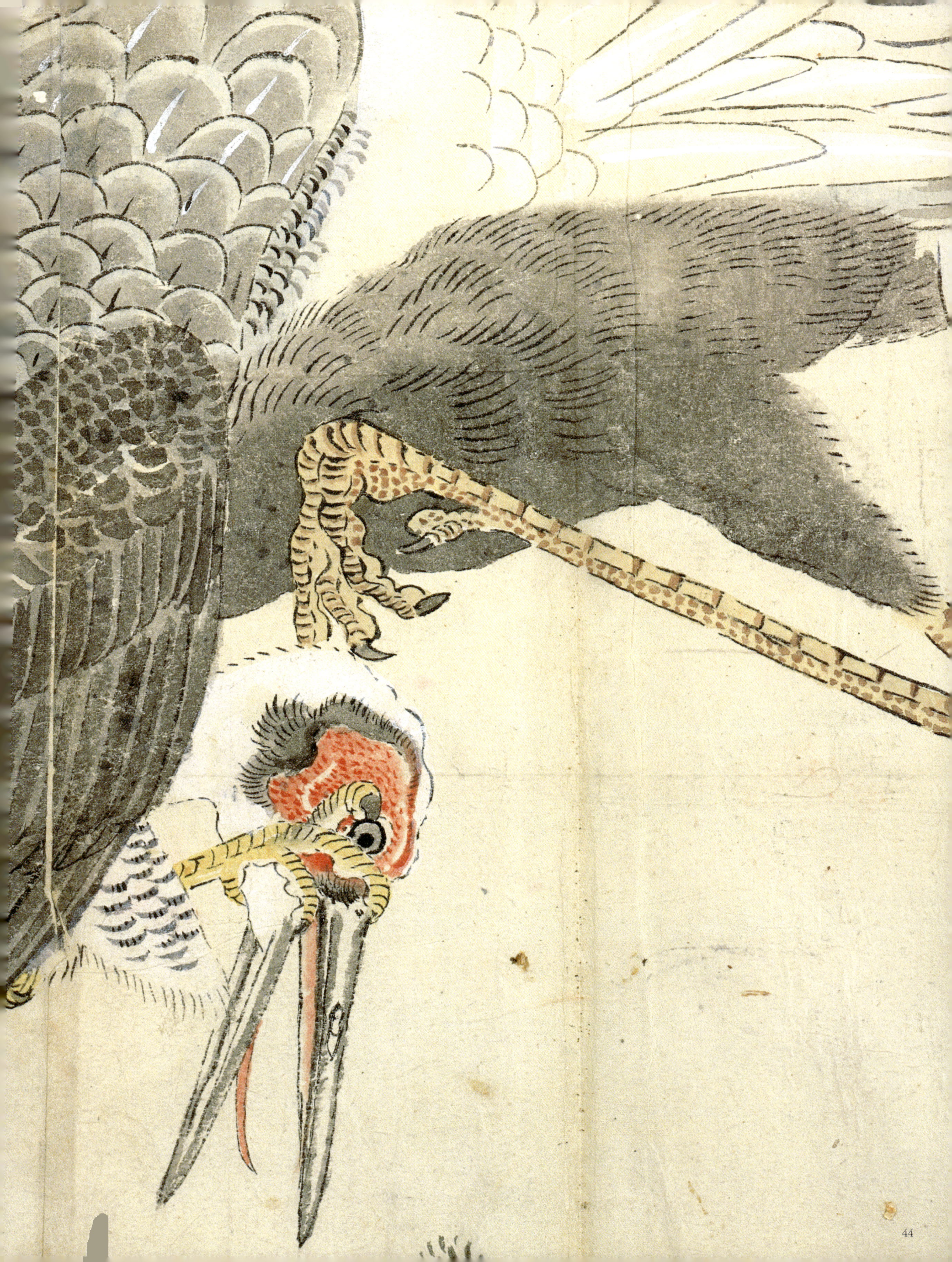

種々図案 | Various Designs

46

種々図案 | Various Designs

48

種々図案 | Various Designs

50

種々図案 | Various Designs

52

種々図案 | VARIOUS DESIGNS

翡翠

魚狗　鵁
キョリ　ヒスイ
美名　カハセミ

一樣筆

飛羽翠

種々図案 | VARIOUS DESIGNS

金色陰月赤銅
器一 黒四分一

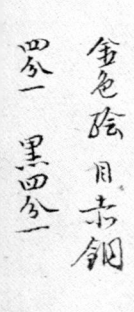

56

種々図案 | Various Designs

58

種々図案 | Various Designs

59

60

せの中みの毛
左右へつる
一寸ニて
十七八本

62

種々図案 | Various Designs

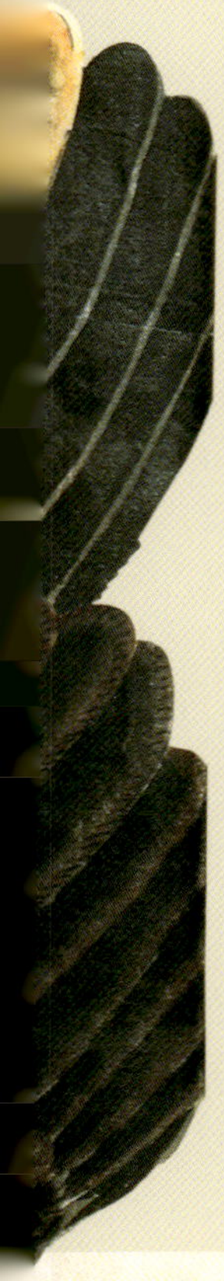

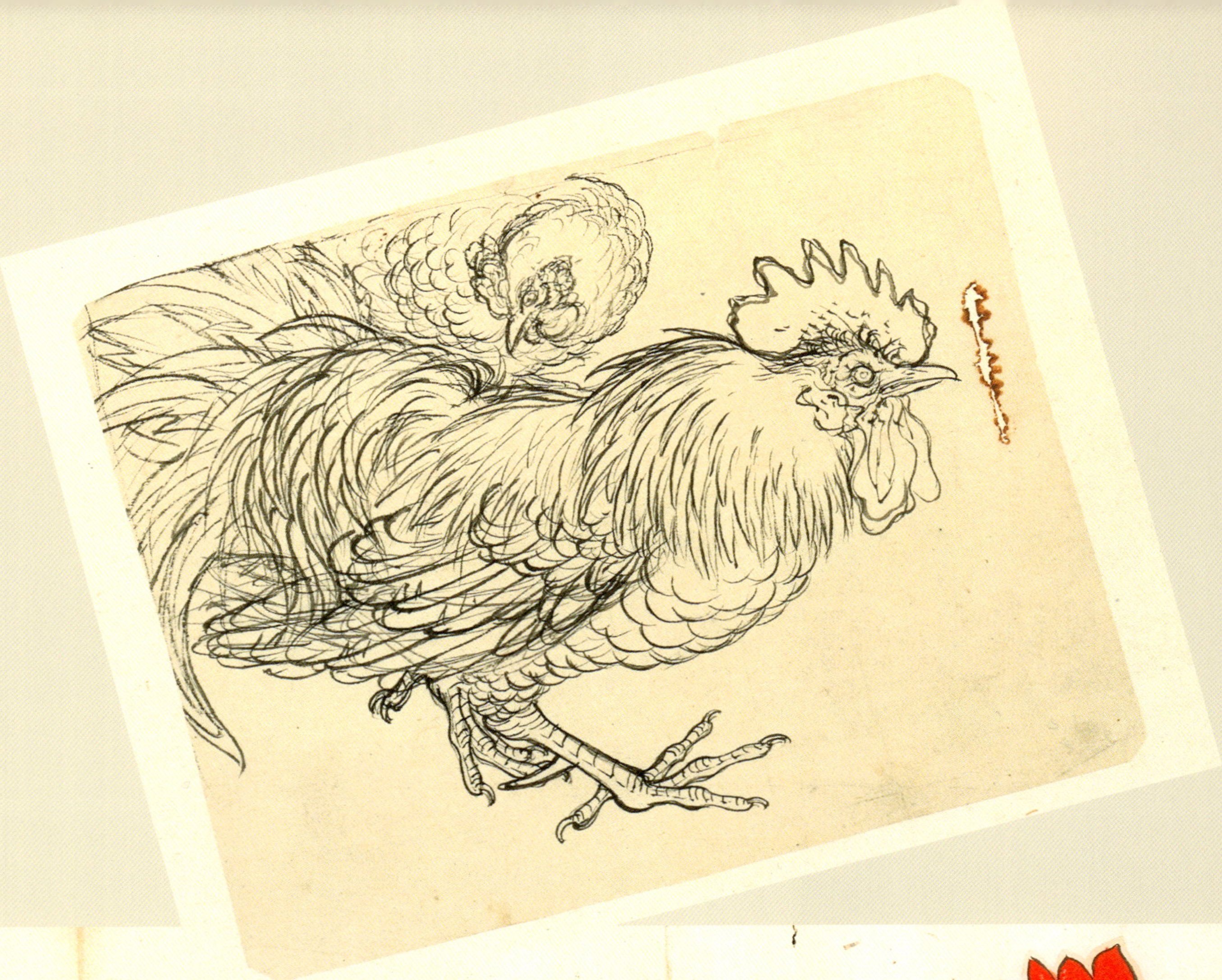

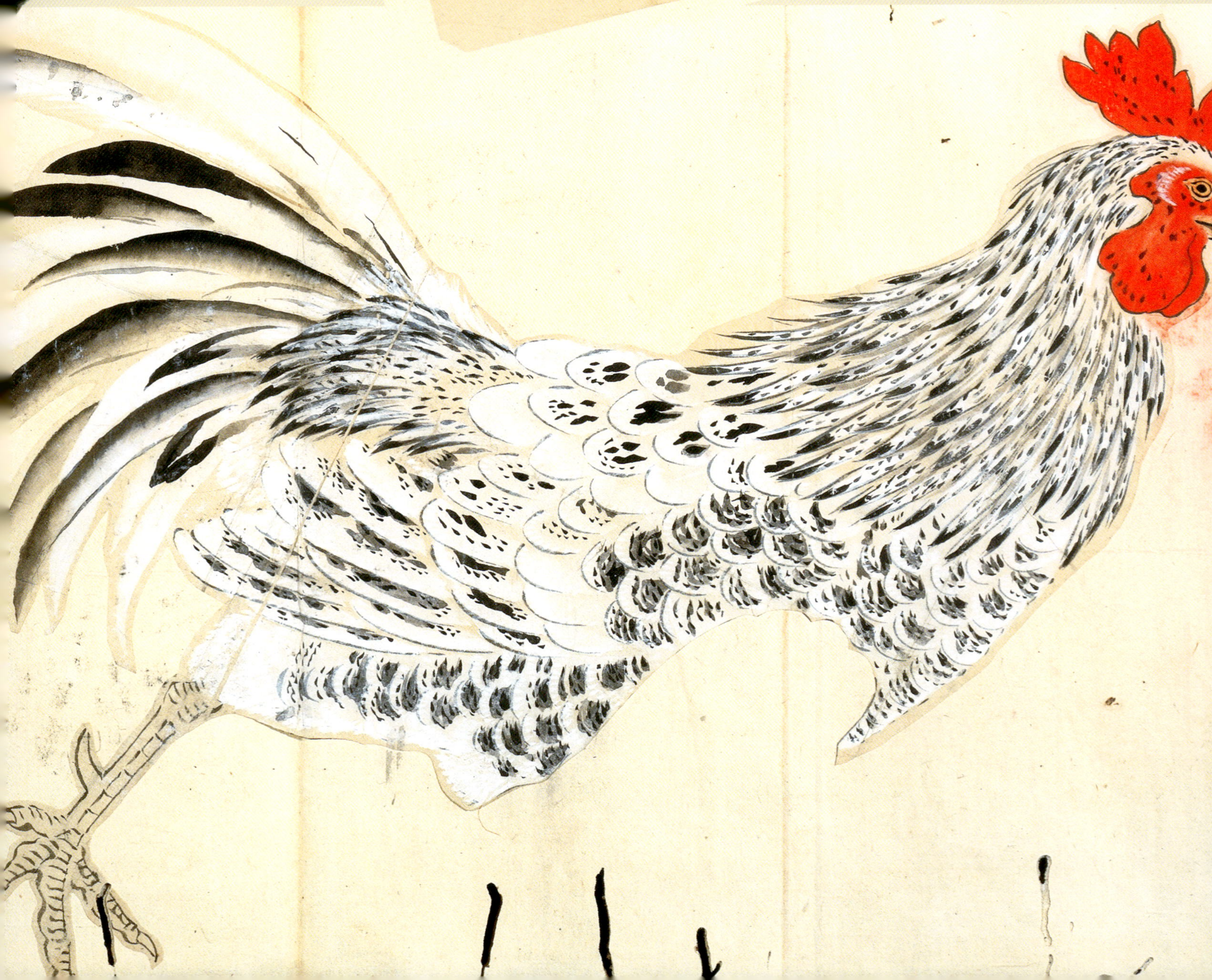

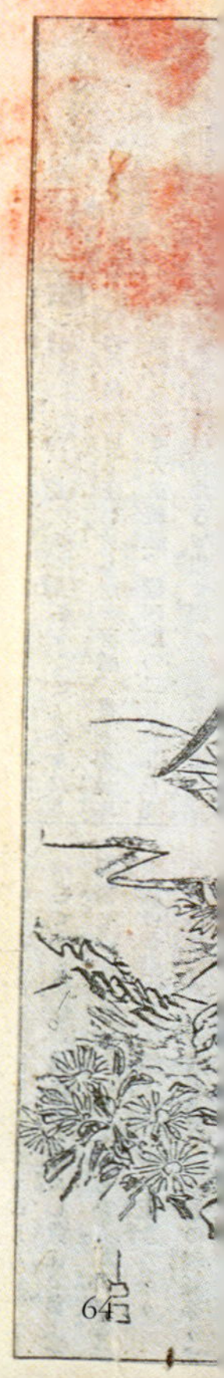
64

種々図案 | Various Designs

福地復一回按
網引図

種々図案 | Various Designs

67

68

種々図案 | VARIOUS DESIGNS

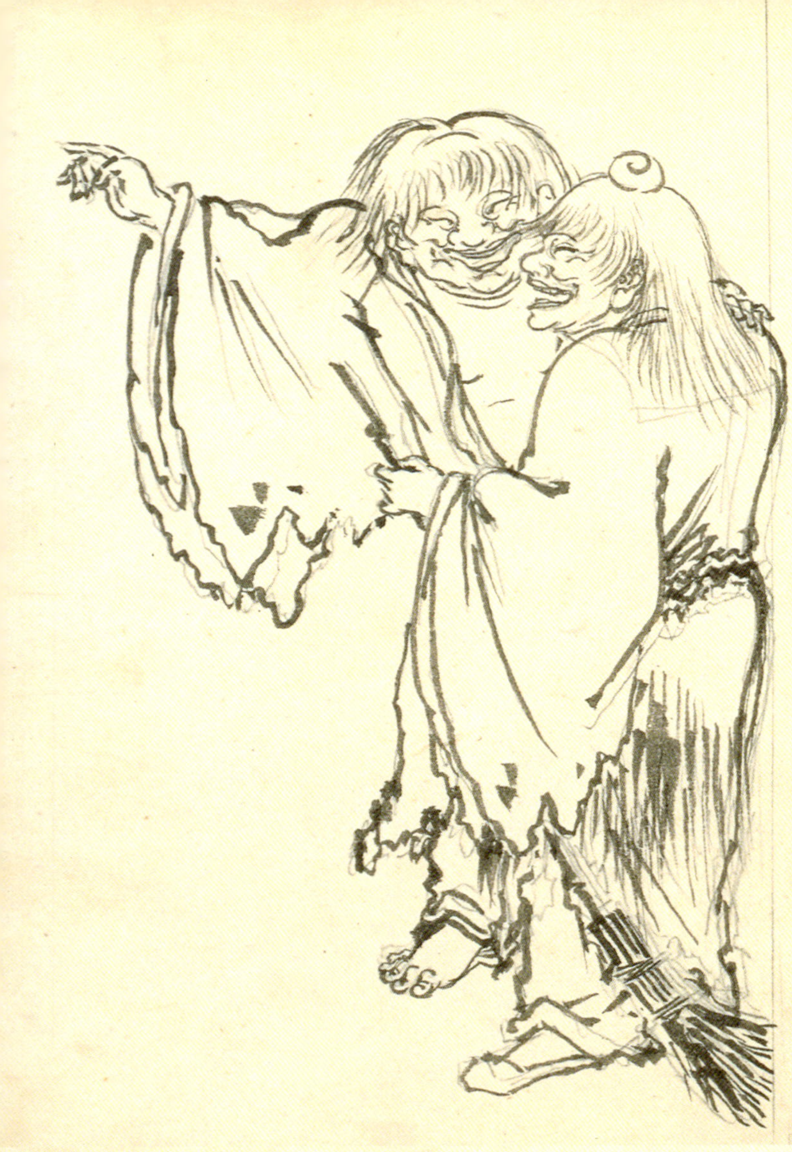
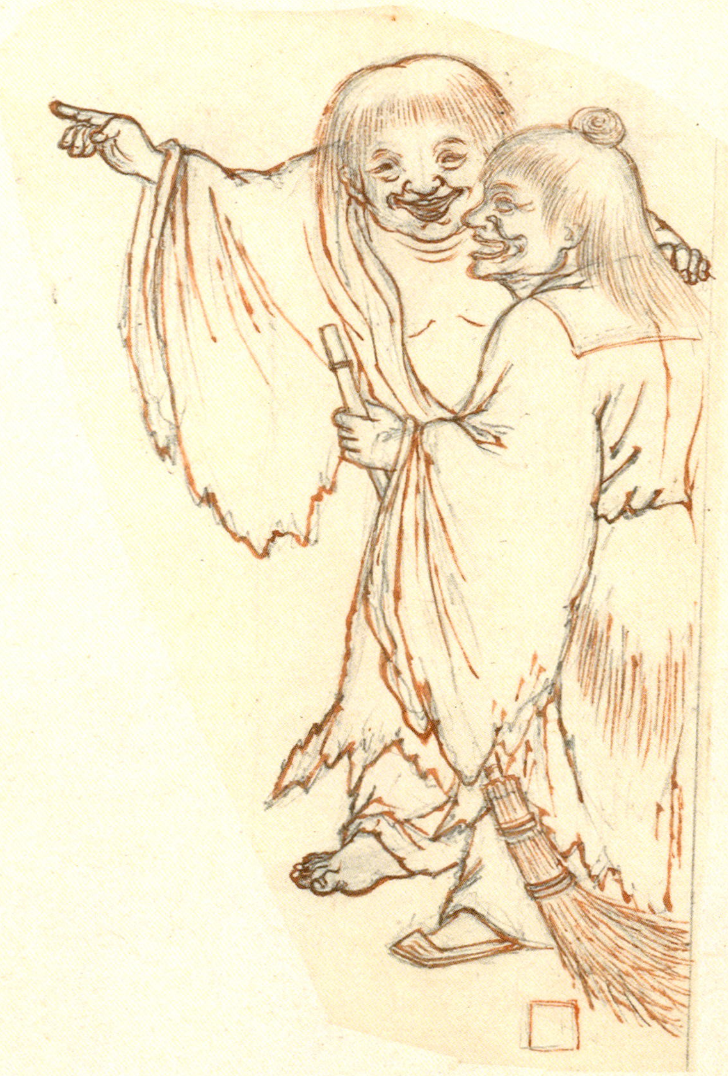
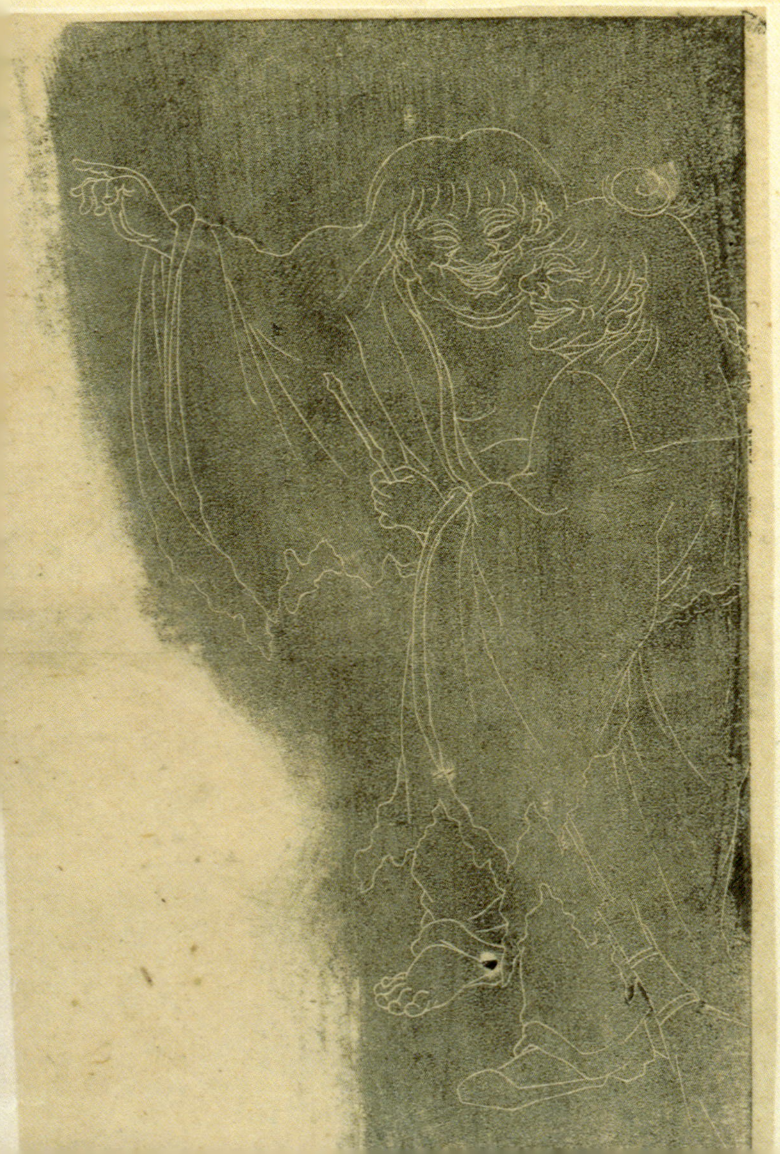
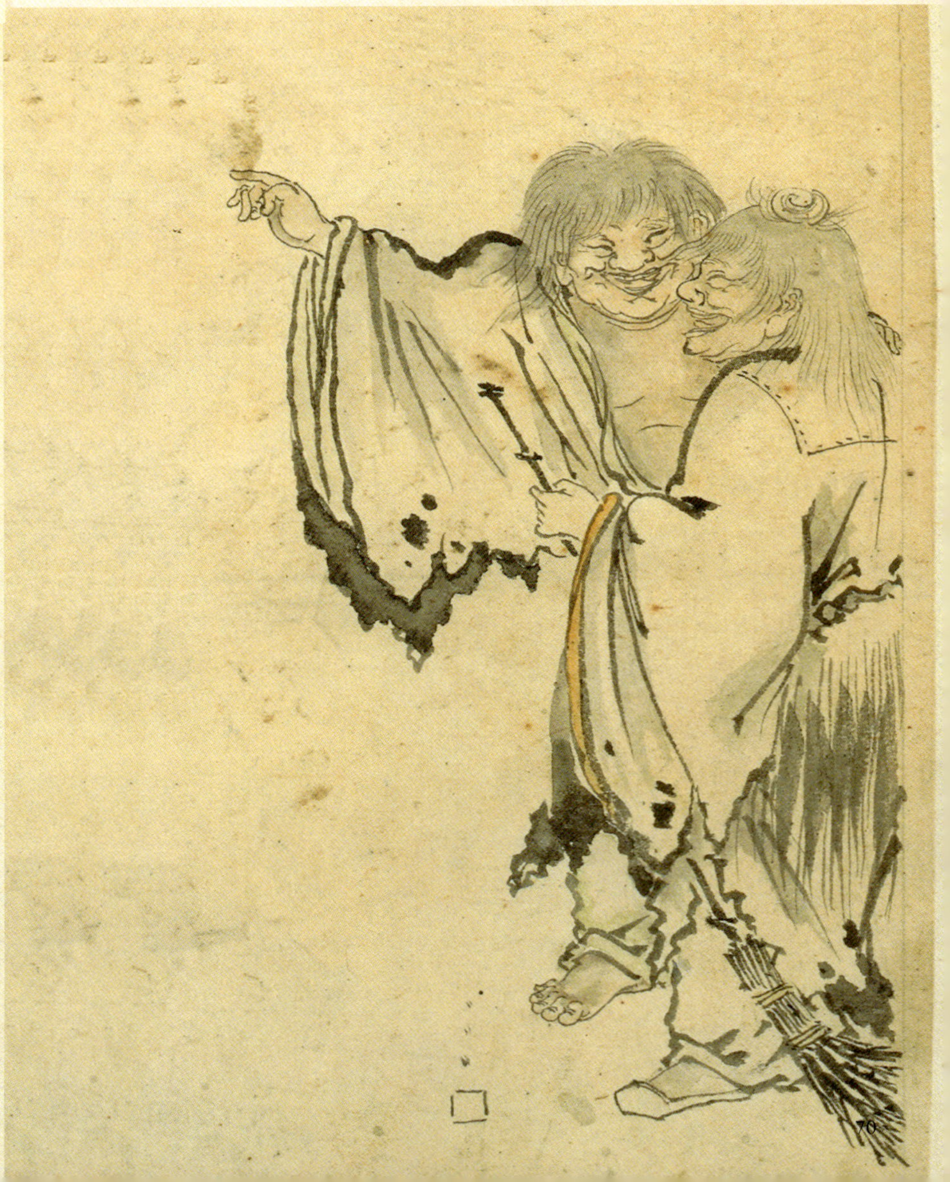

種々図案

Various Designs

小面

71

72

種々図案 | Various Designs

74

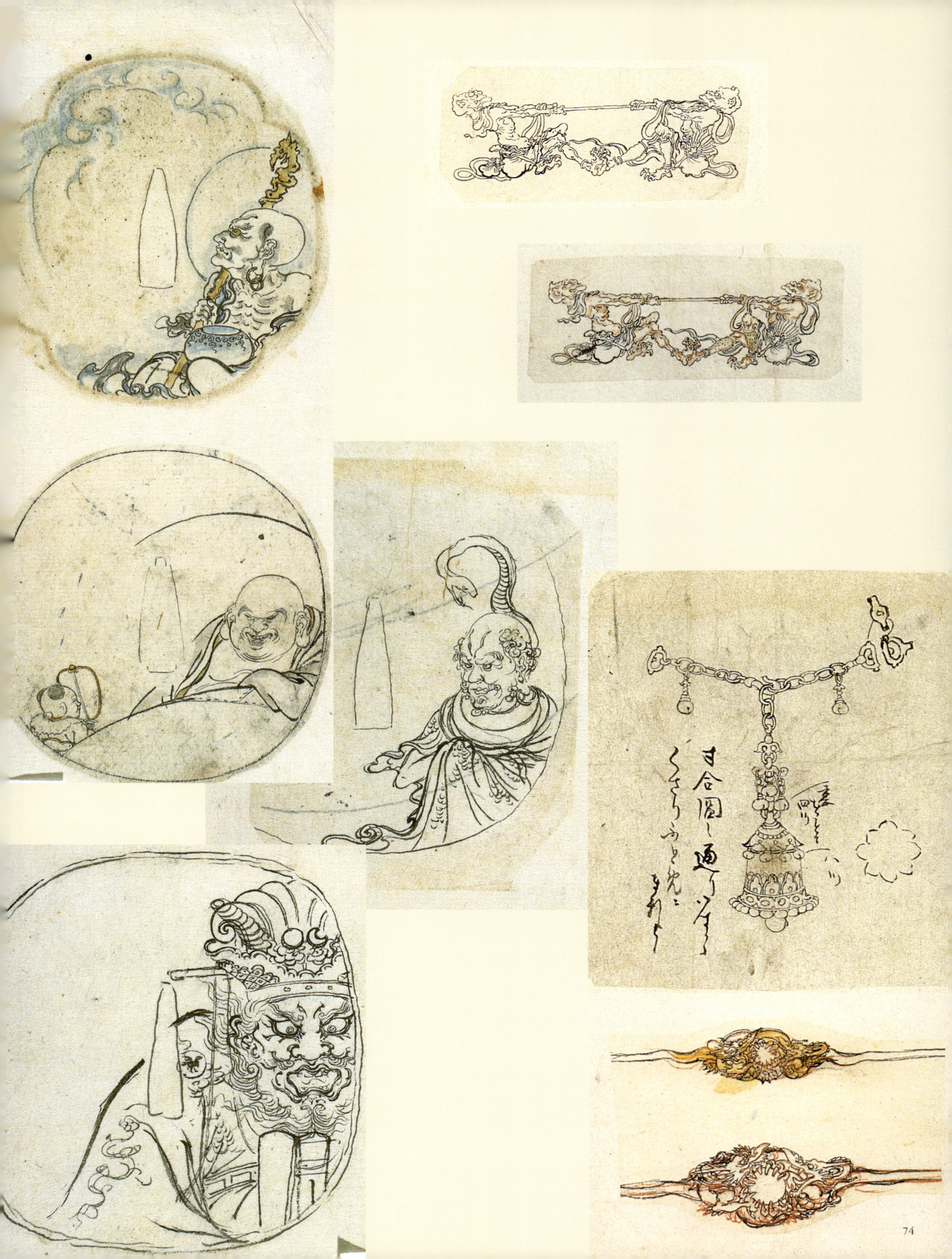

種々図案 | Various Designs

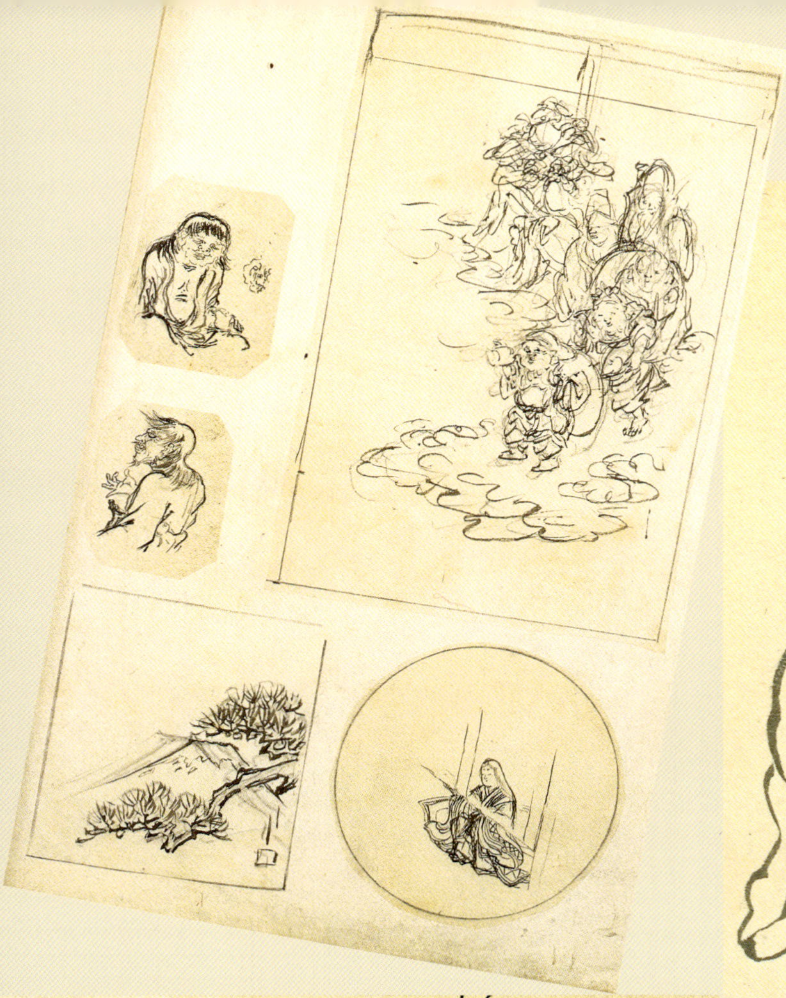

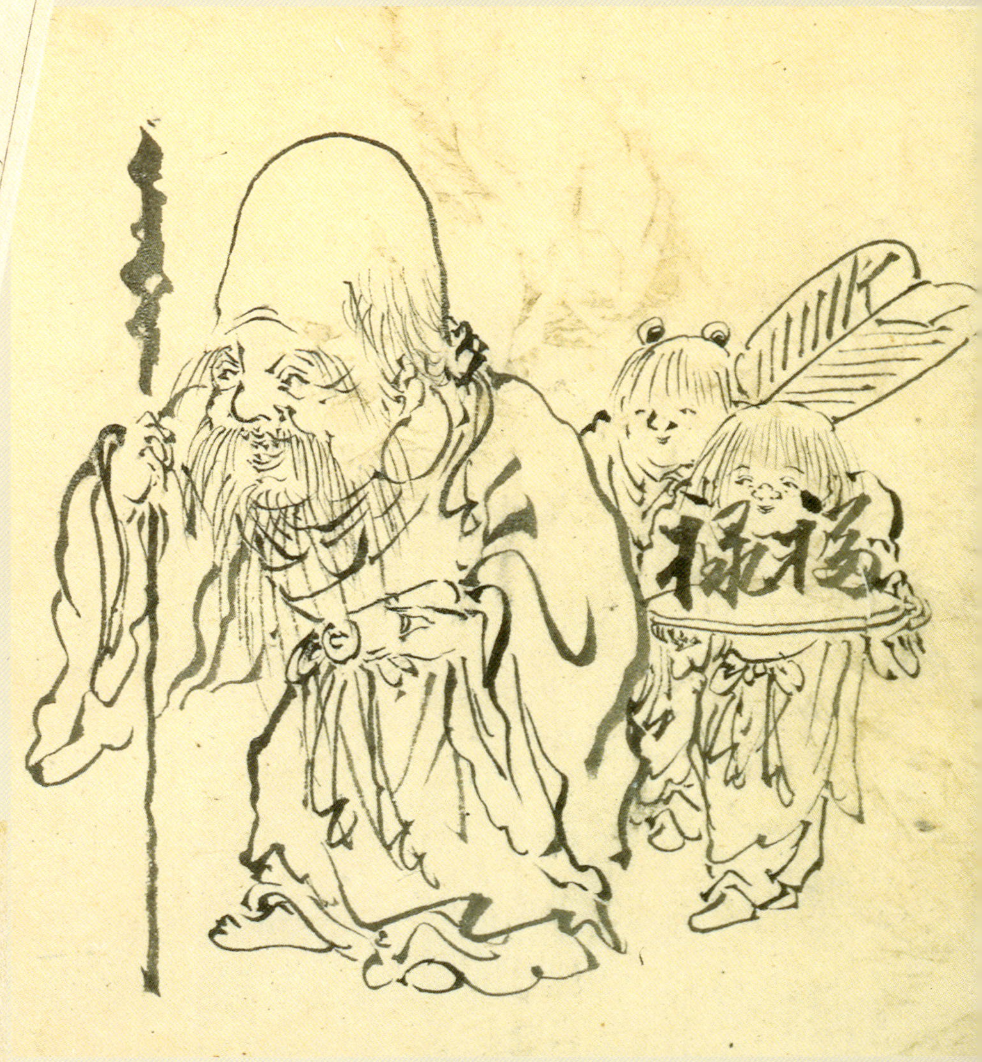

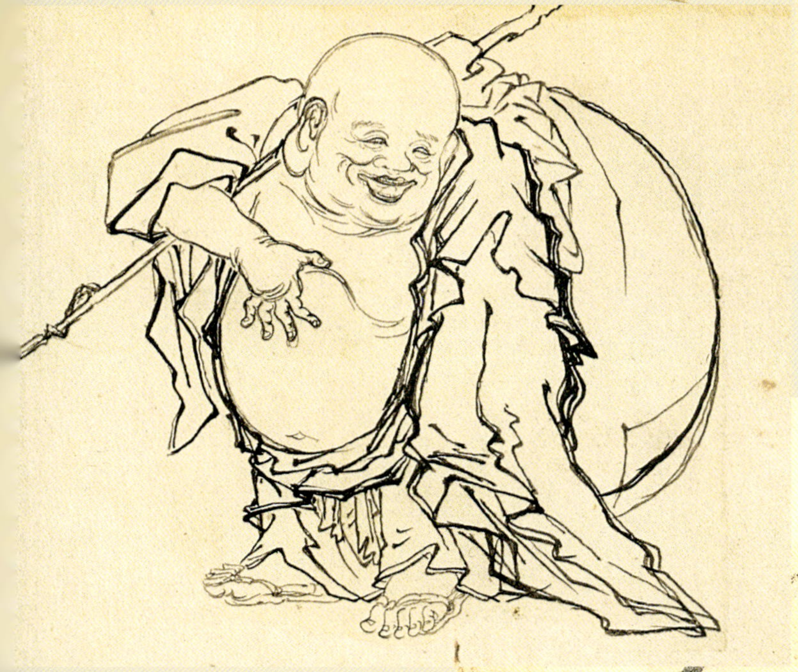

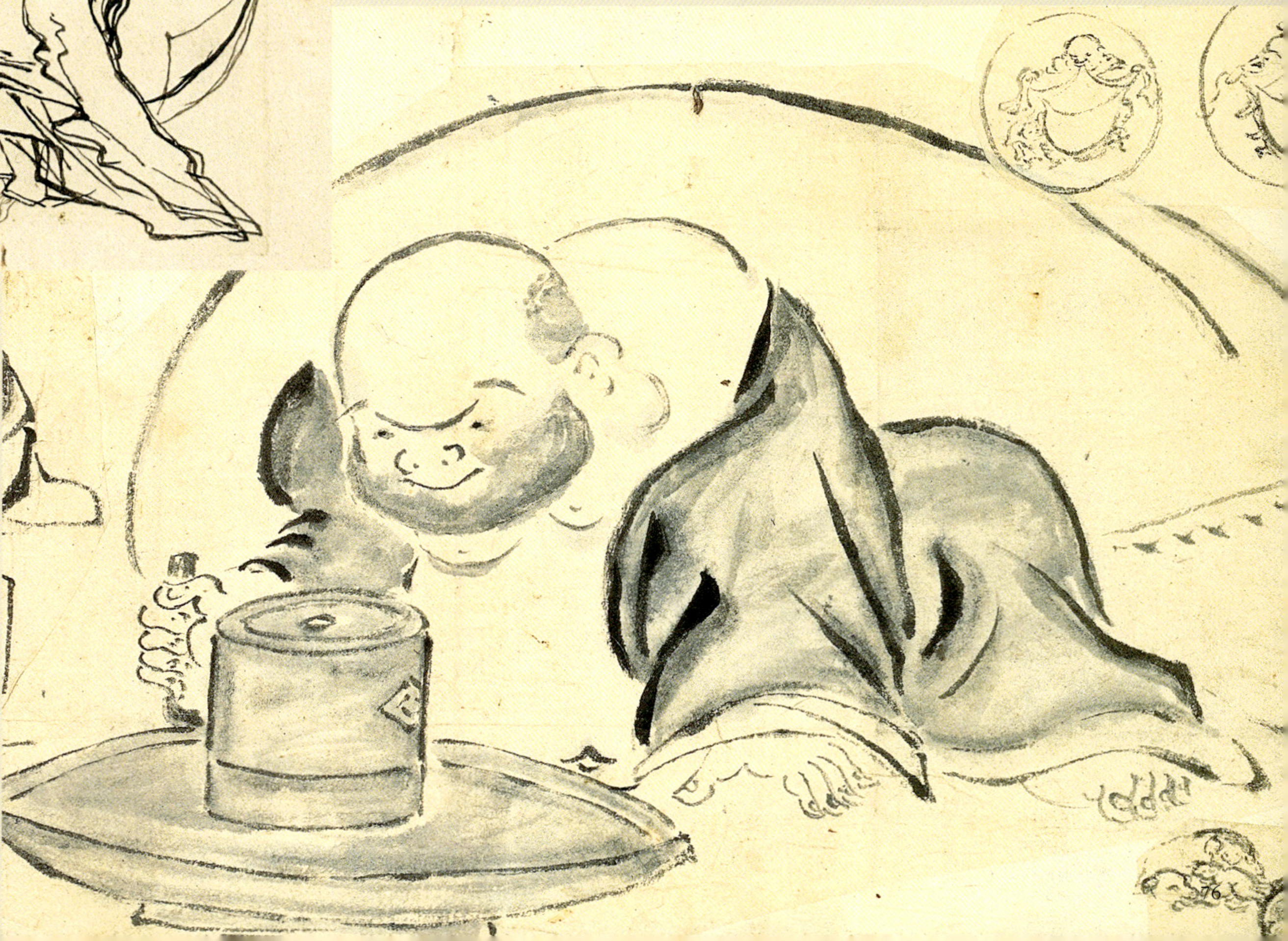

種々図案 | Various Designs

78

種々図案 | Various Designs

文昌星古図

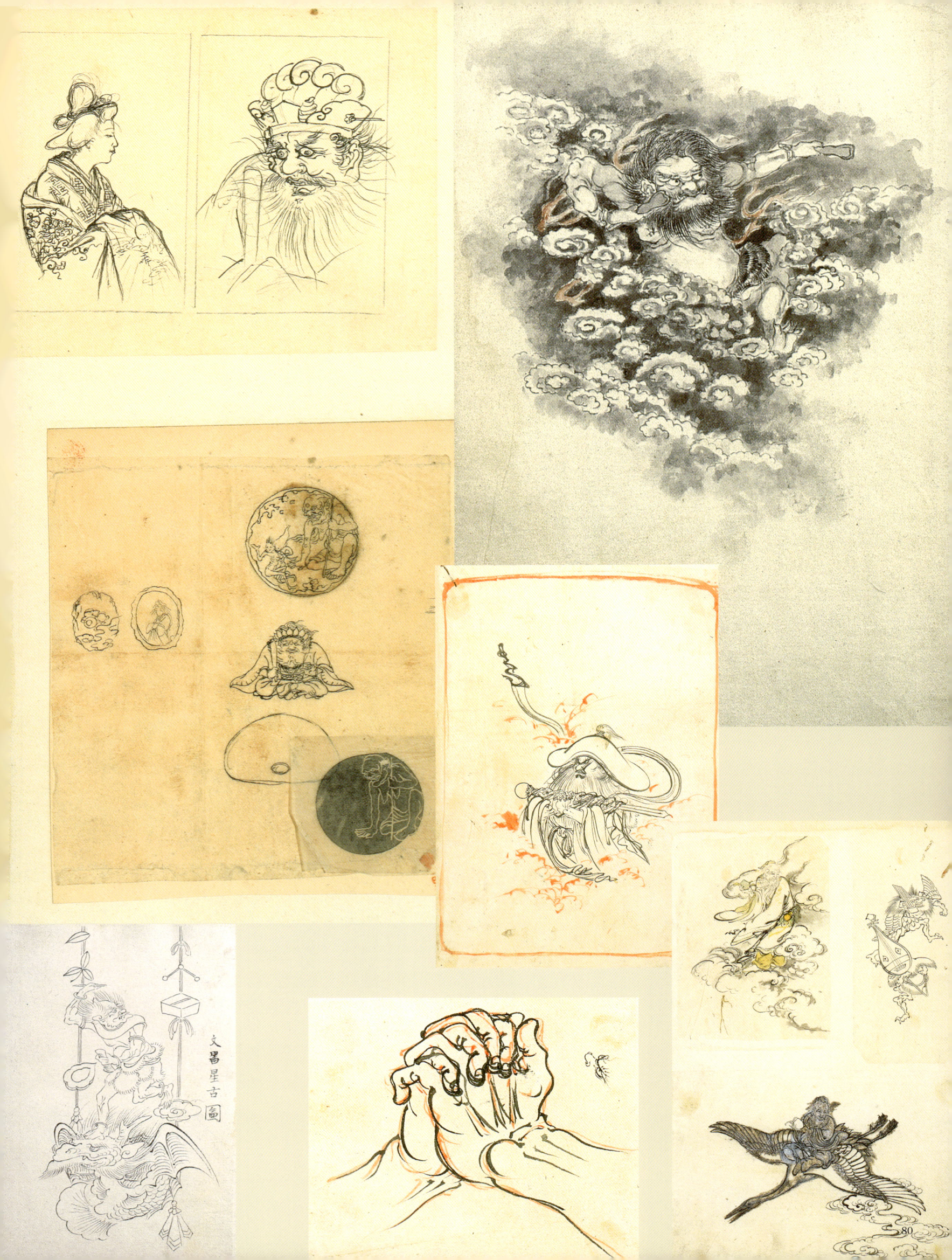

種々図案 | VARIOUS DESIGNS

水戸家重宝文昌星原品 犬八寸餘上青銅鋳物摸擬蔣銘龍 画盖 雲衫 鷓錺之

81

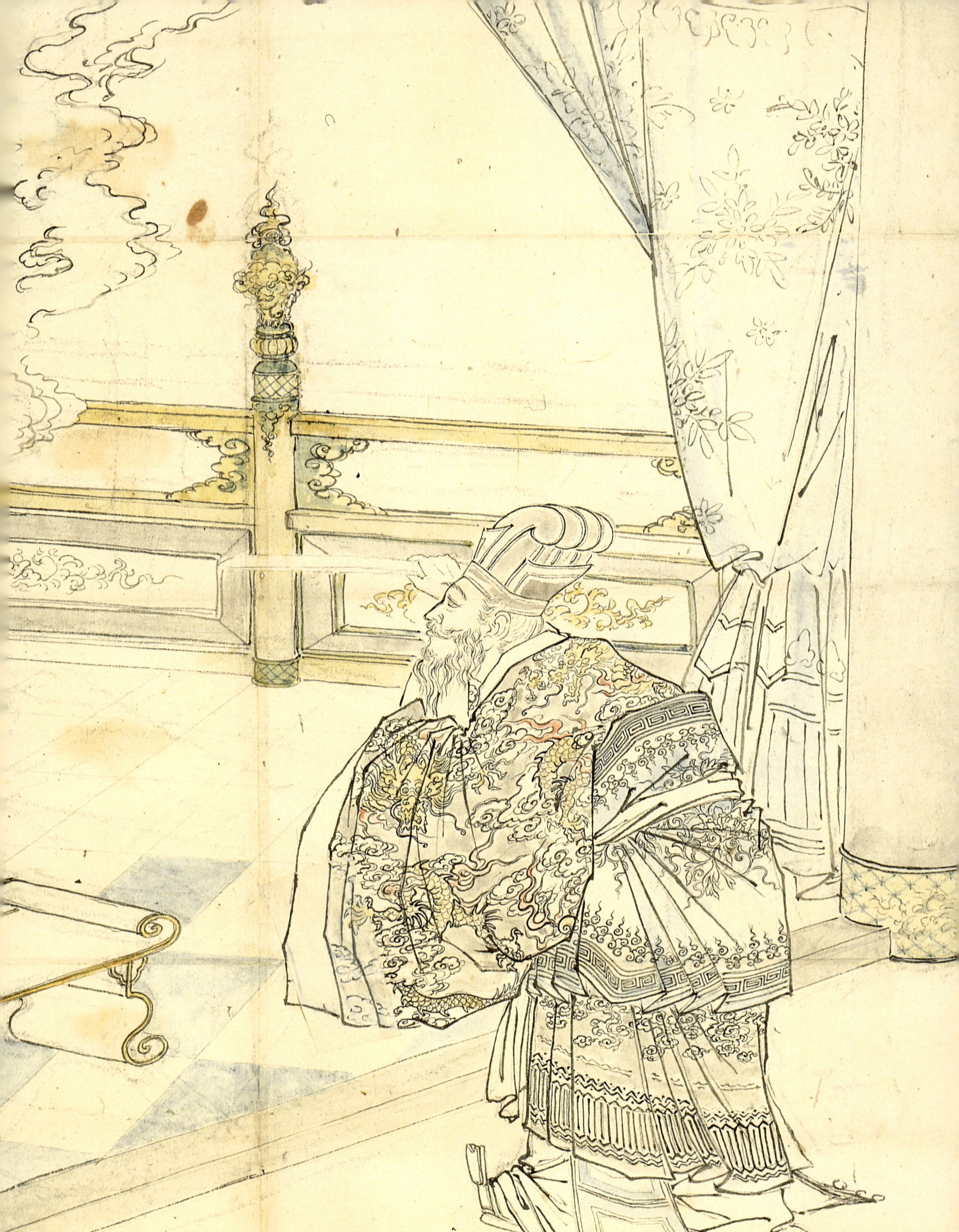

種々図案 | Various Designs

83

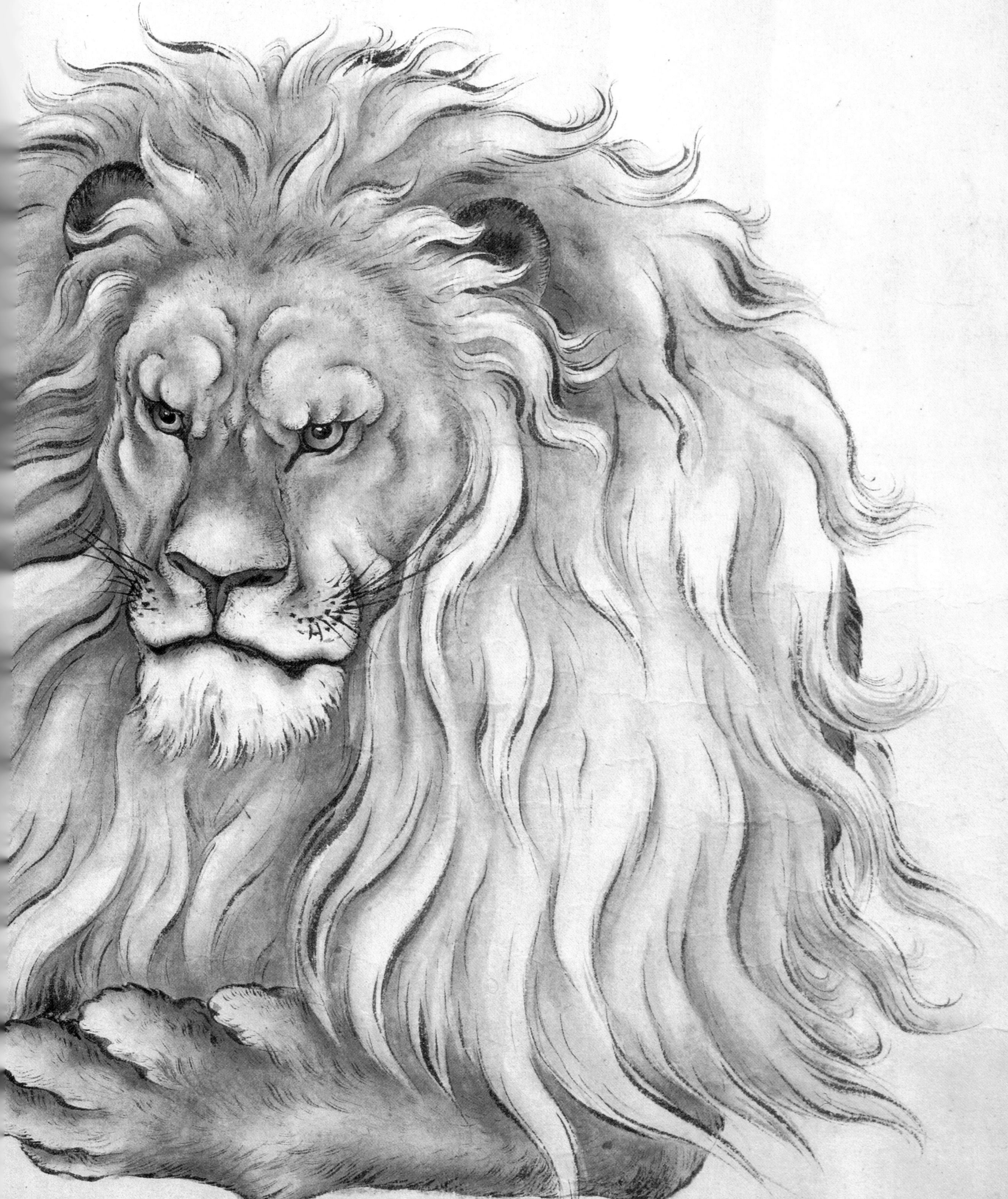

種々図案 | Various Designs

86

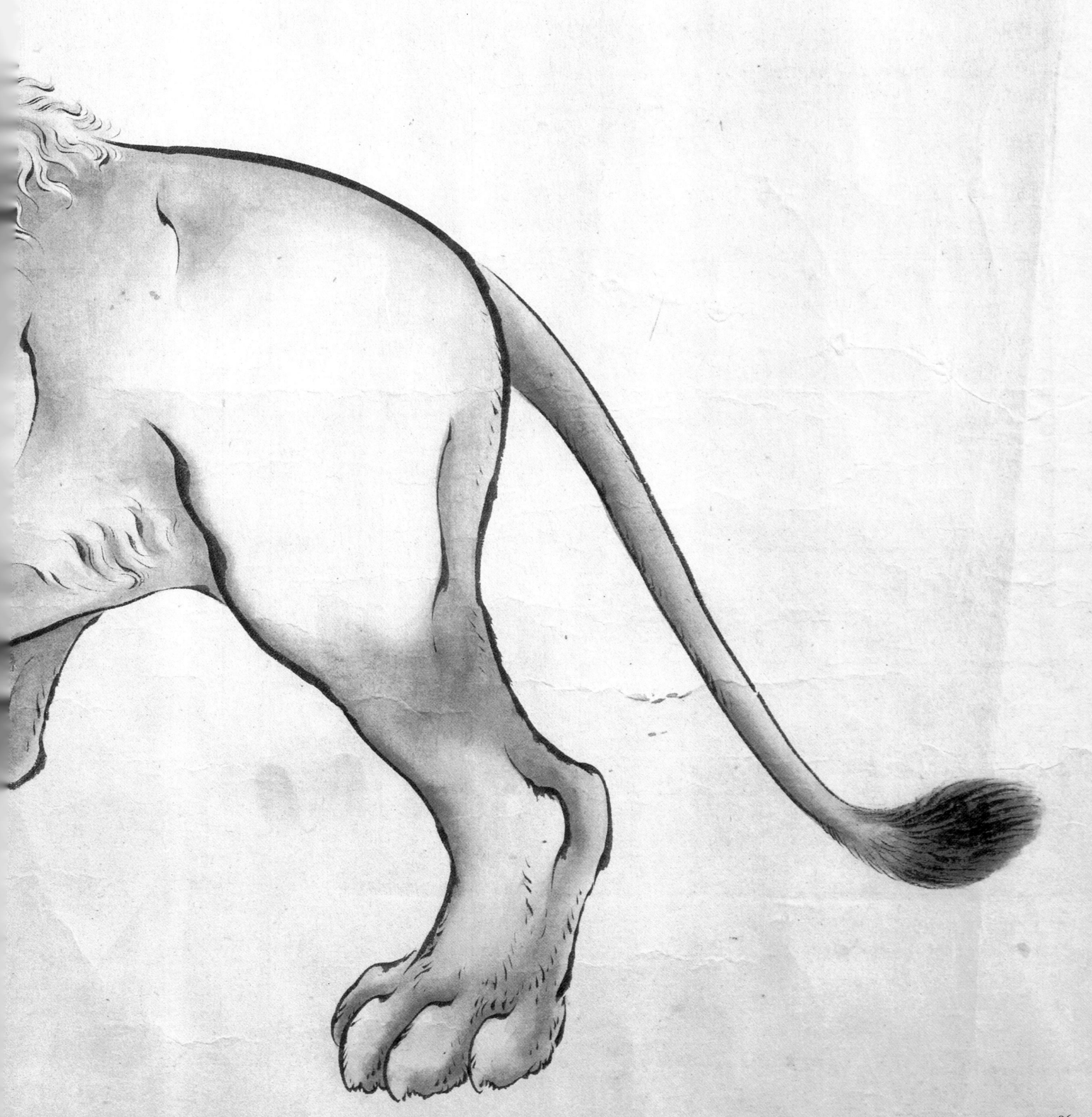

種々図案 | Various Designs

獅子之圖

種々図案 | VARIOUS DESIGNS

90

種々図案 | Various Designs

92

種々図案 | Various Designs

93

94

種々図案 | Various Designs

香爐金銀彫鏤

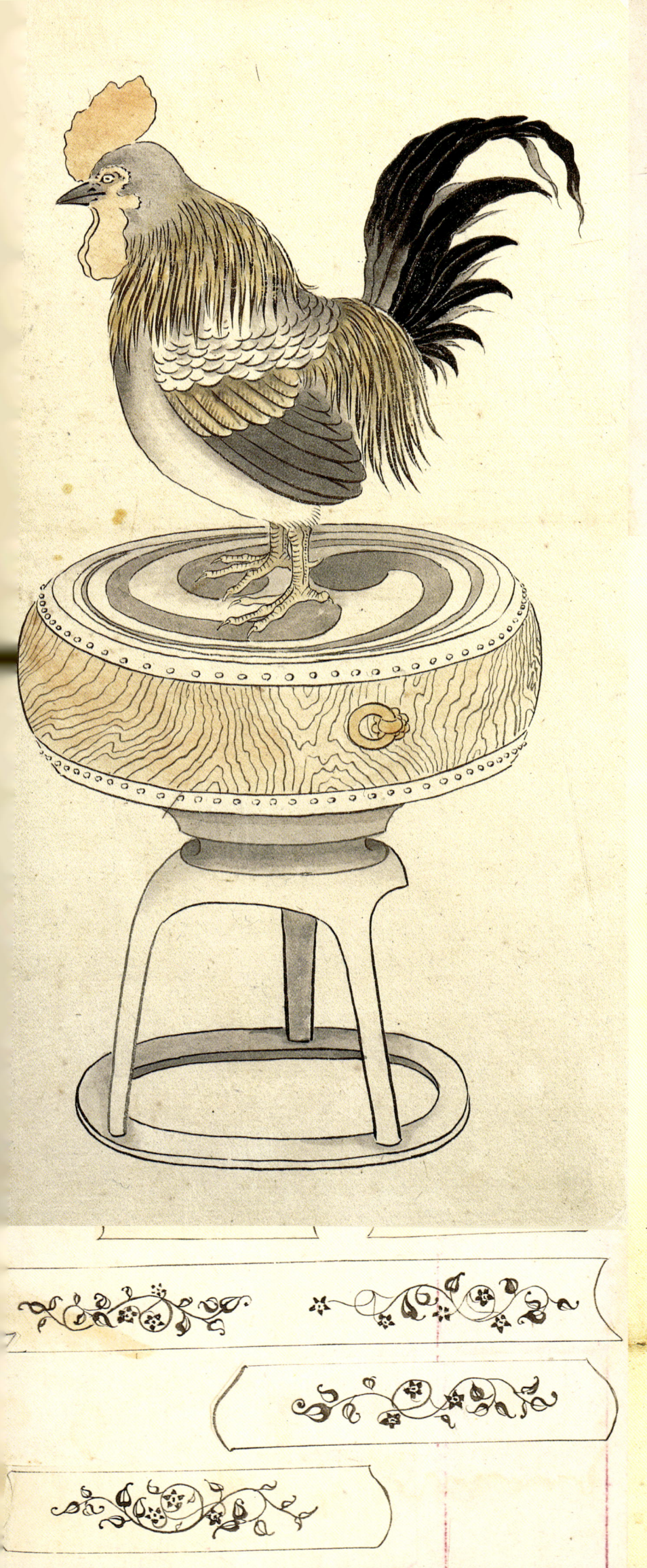

鈎銀製尾赤銅
口少足入金上廿分銅

太鼓取聚
模様薄肉
鈞金景眼入

臺赤銅製
面四分一
小振力七唐草入金象嵌
篤銅四分一金銀

鈎銀製足入金
上廿分銅

小菊　黄菊白菊　花紅葉　藤牡丹　梅　桂花

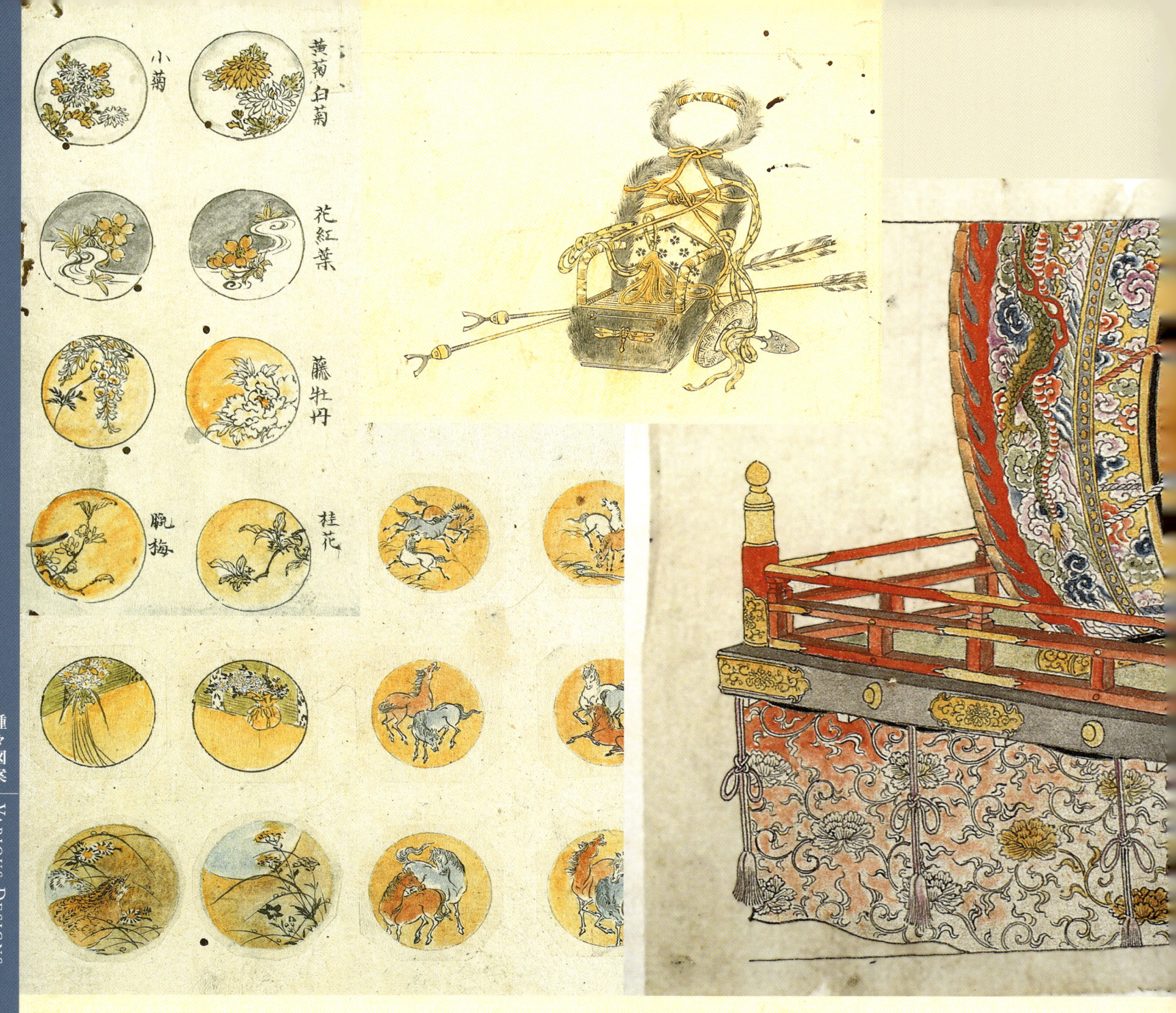

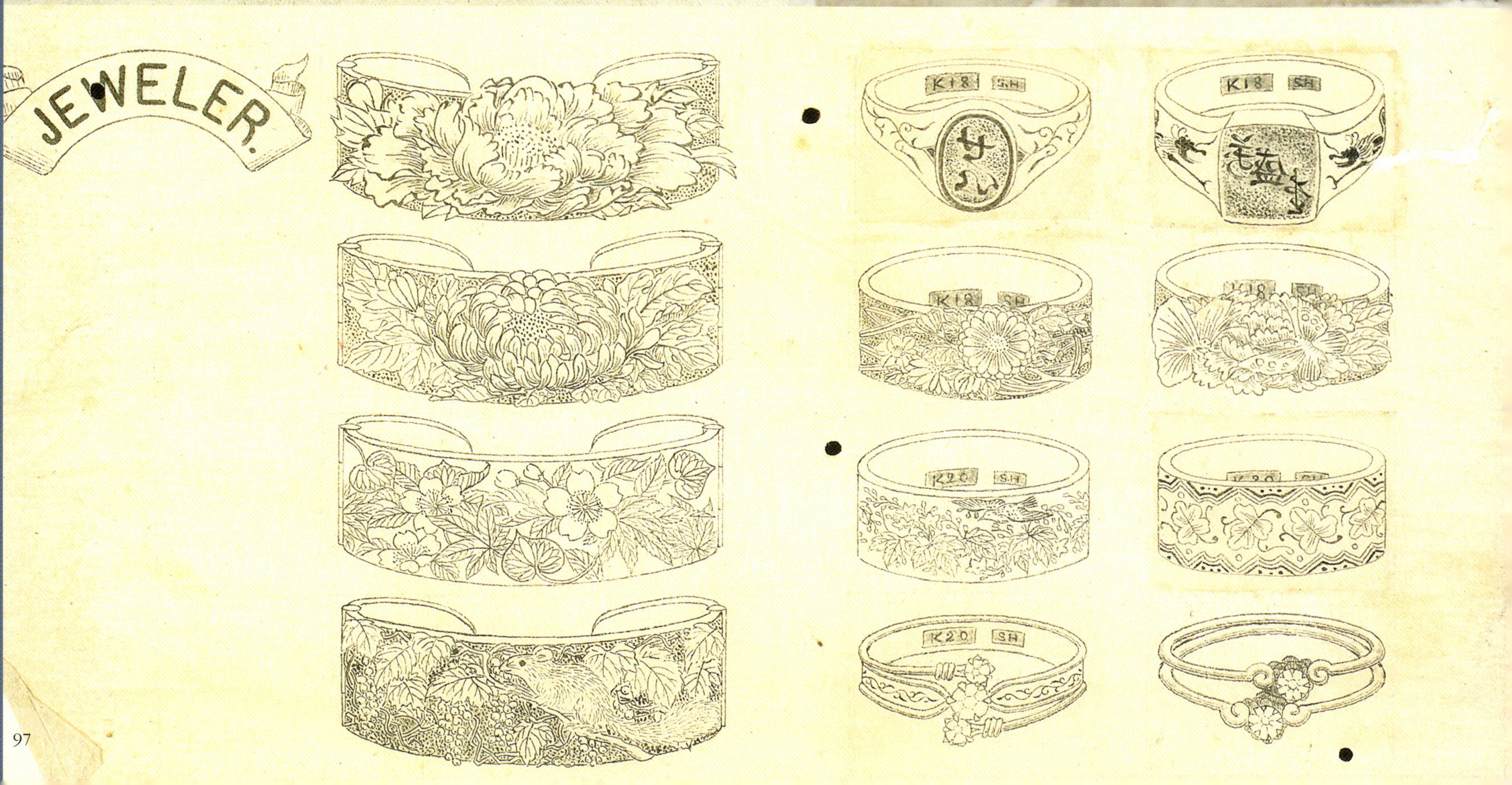

JEWELER.

種々図案 | Various Designs

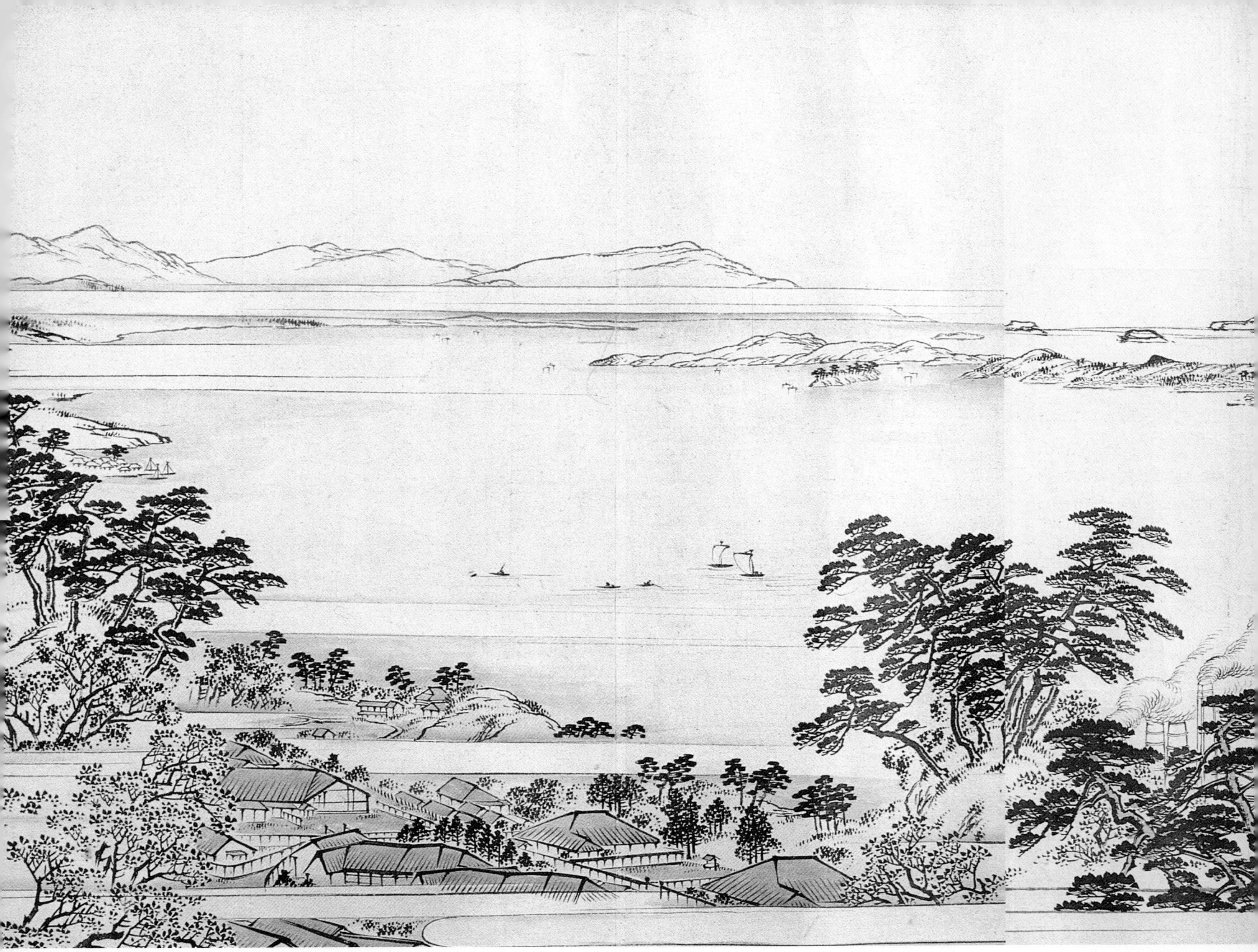

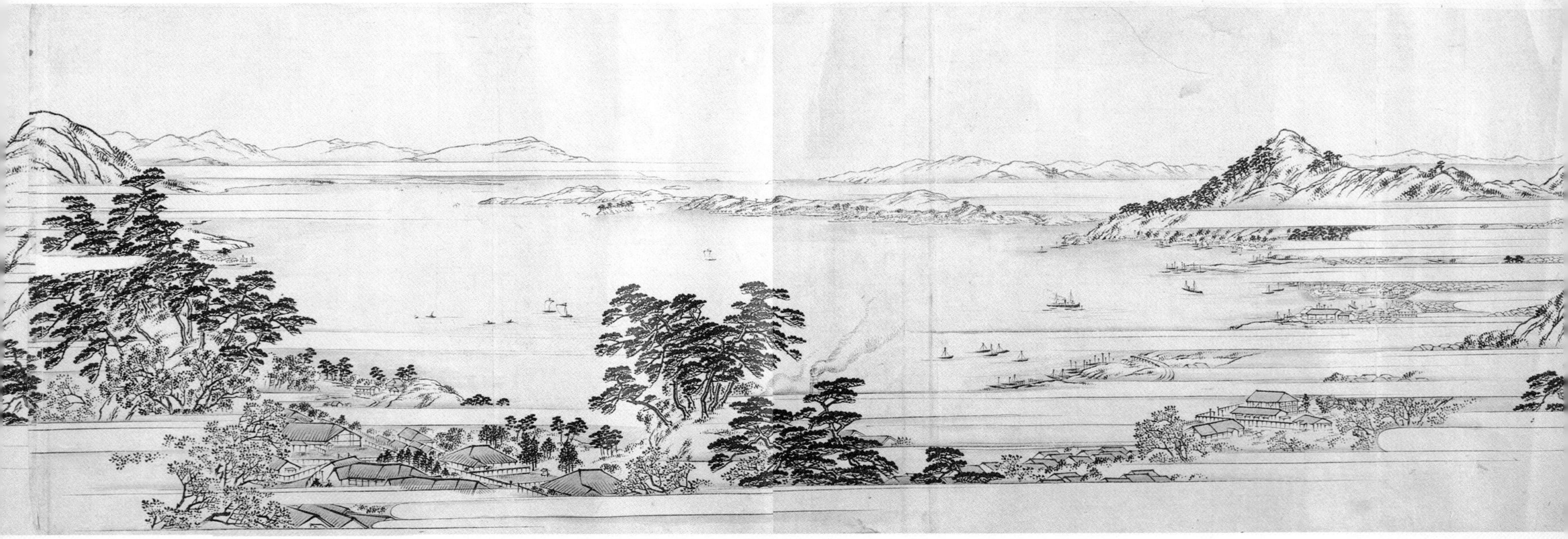

種々図案 | Various Designs

蘆雪ハ 桃今き夏ん金ら
の上六文ハ 平多象殿ゝ総ん
千巴入る箱 又ハ庄切文ろい
あ然

100

種々図案 | VARIOUS DESIGNS

月之圖　日之圖

102

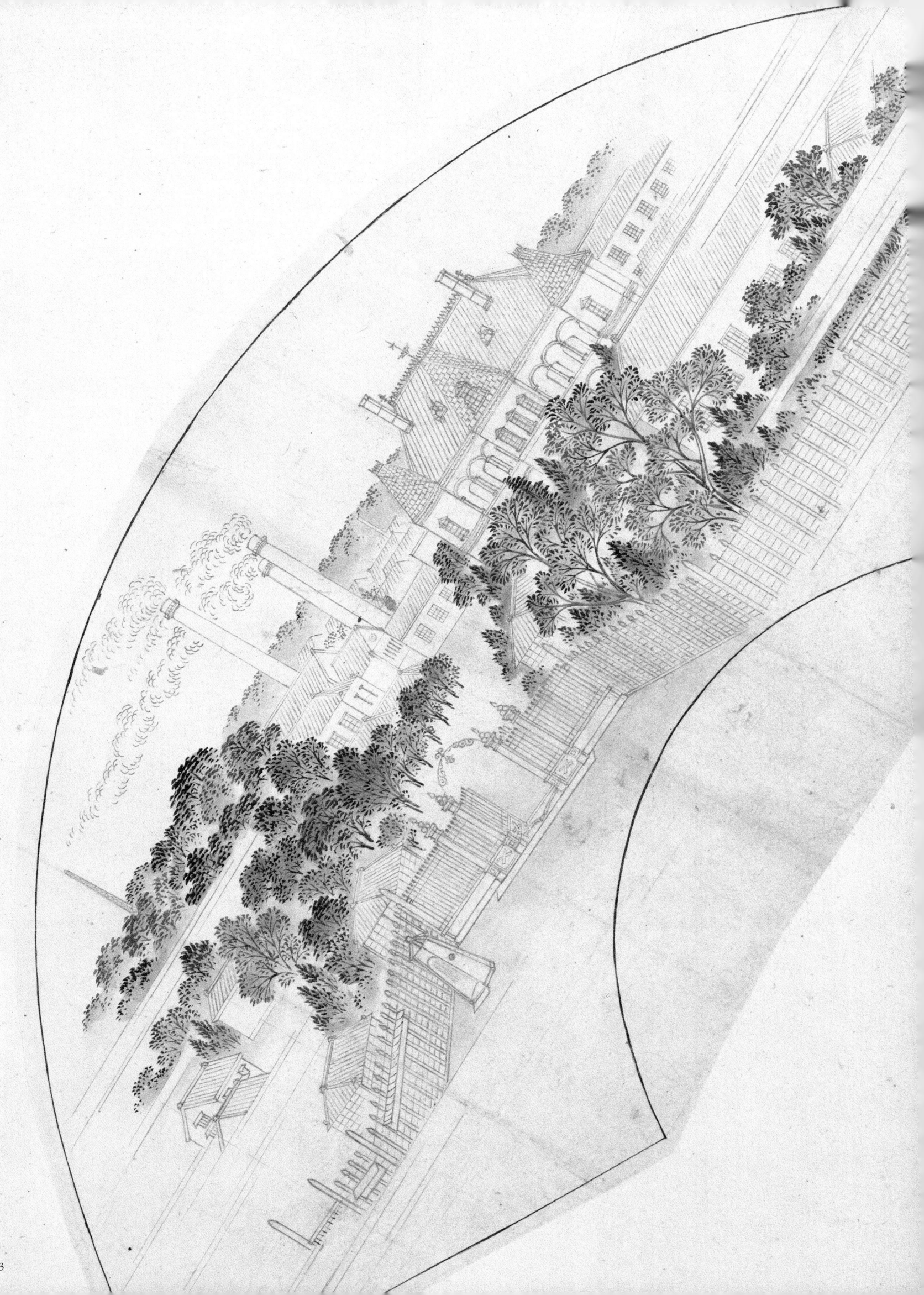

種々図案 | Various Designs

104

手板・煙草入

手板は東京美術学校の彫金の教程の見本として海野勝珉が制作し、昭和初期まで数多くの学生が模刻した作品である。煙草入は東京芸術大学大学美術館のコレクションの中で唯一の海野勝珉による完成作であり、該当する図案のみならず、類似する構図の図案も少なくない。

Metalwork Plates & Cigarette Case

The metalwork plates were created by Unno Shomin as models for learning metal carving techniques in the Tokyo Fine Art School, and many students studied them making copies until the early Showa period. The cigarette case is the only completed work within The University Art Museum, Tokyo National University of Fine Arts and Music collection, and its design sketch and similar sketches are also in the collection.

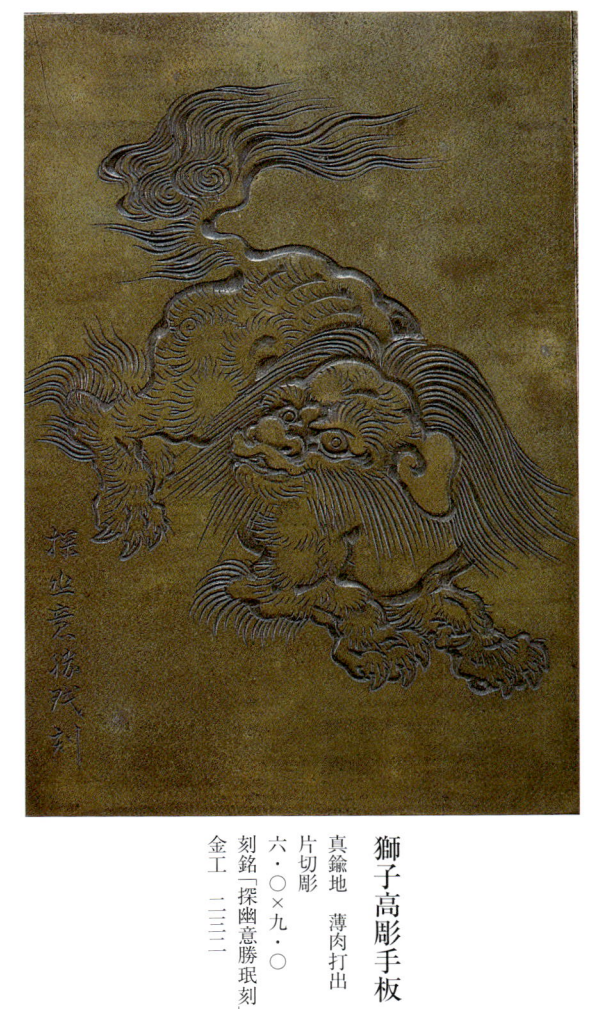

キリン彫手板
四分一地　薄肉打出
片切彫
九・一×六・〇五
刻銘「東京美術學校
教授芳洲海野勝珉鐫」
金工　三二三

獅子高彫手板
真鍮地　薄肉打出
片切彫
六・〇×九・〇
刻銘「探幽意勝珉刻」
金工　三二二

拾得手板
四分一地　肉合彫
六・一×九・一
刻銘「勝珉」花押
金工　三二五

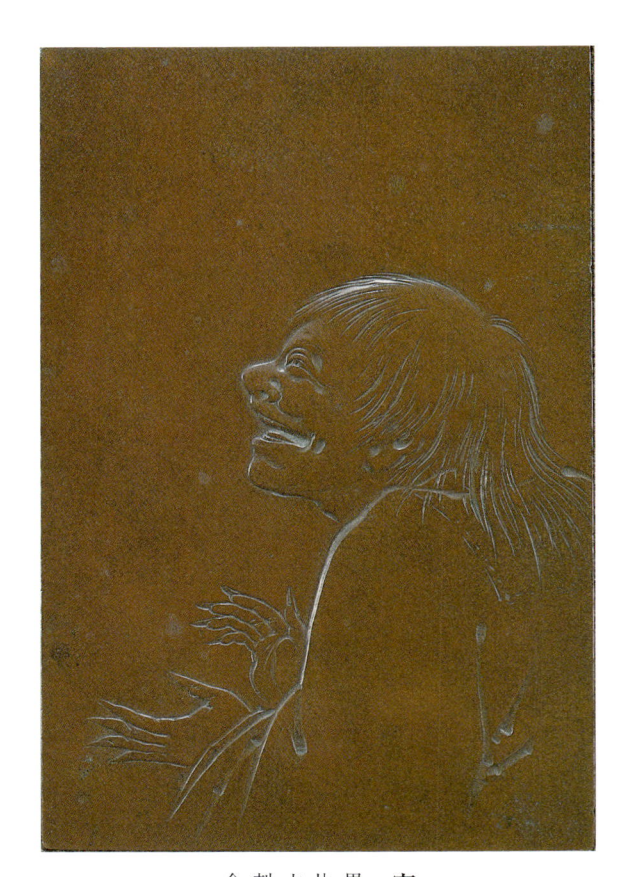

寒山手板
黒味銅地　薄肉打出
片切彫　毛彫
六・一×九・一
刻銘「勝珉」花押
金工　三二四

106

手板・煙草入 | METALWORK PLATES & CIGARETTE CASE

狐手板
四分一地　薄肉打出
金・銀象嵌
片切彫
六・二×九・二
刻銘「勝珉刻」
金工　三二七

虎手板
真鍮地　薄肉打出
六・〇×九・一
刻銘「李龍眠意勝珉刻」
金工　三二八

雁手板
四分一地　薄肉打出
赤銅象嵌　金色絵
片切彫
六・一×九・一
刻銘「應擧意　勝珉刻」
金工　三二六

芦雁片切彫手板

銅地　片切彫
一五・四×一八・四
刻銘「壬子春之日　勝珉鐵筆」
金工　三八六

雁片切彫手板

銅地　片切彫
一五・四×一八・五
刻銘「壬子春之日　勝珉鐵筆」
金工　三八七

山水片切彫手板
銅地　片切彫
一五・四×一八・五
刻銘「芳洲迂士勝珉」
金工　三八八

芭蕉片切彫手板
銅地　片切彫　金象嵌
一五・四×一八・五
刻銘「芳洲海野勝珉」
金工　三八九

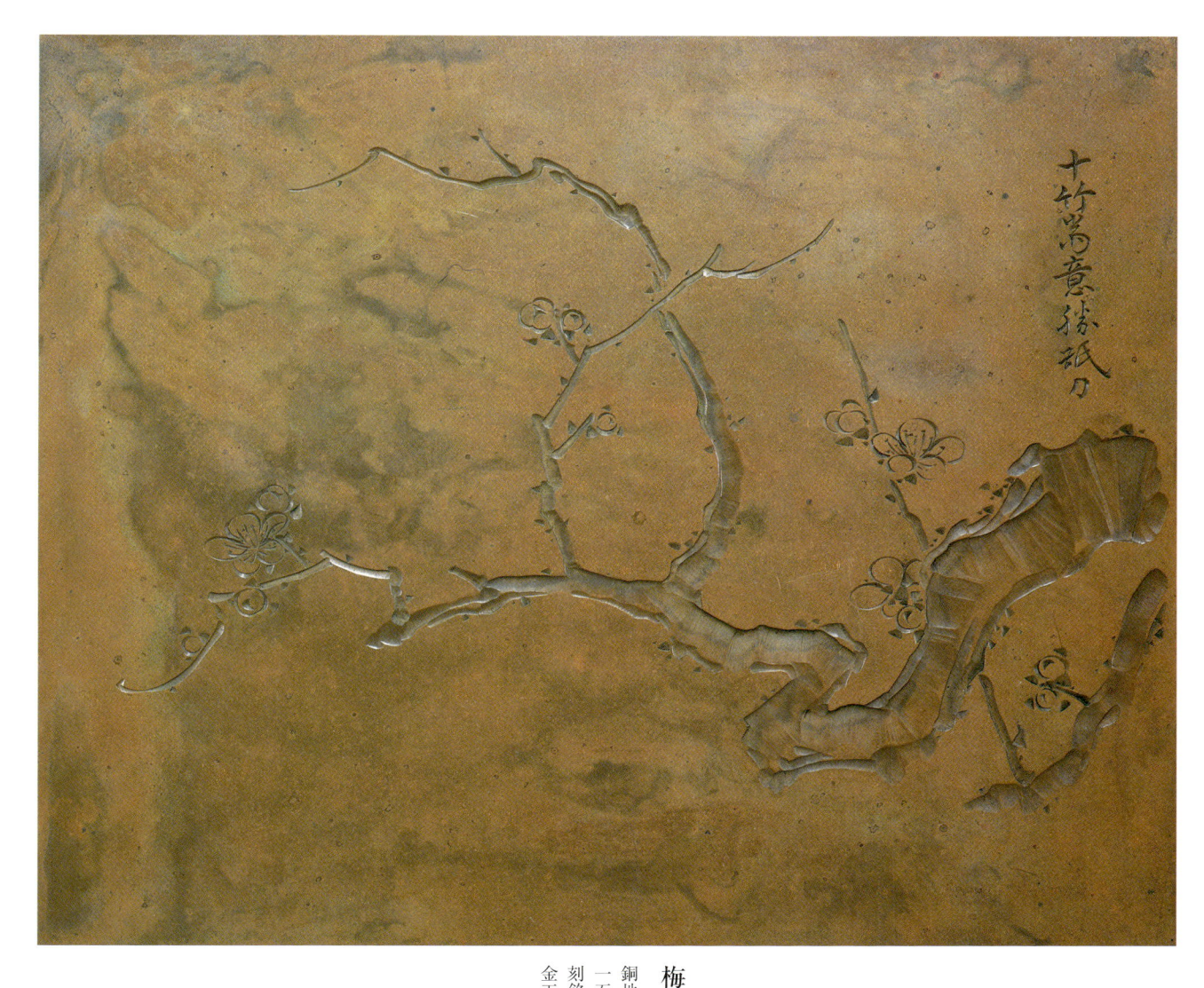

手板・煙草入 | Metalwork Plates & Cigarette Case

梅樹片切彫手板

銅地　片切彫
一五・四×一八・五
刻銘「十竹翁意勝珉刀」
金工　三九〇

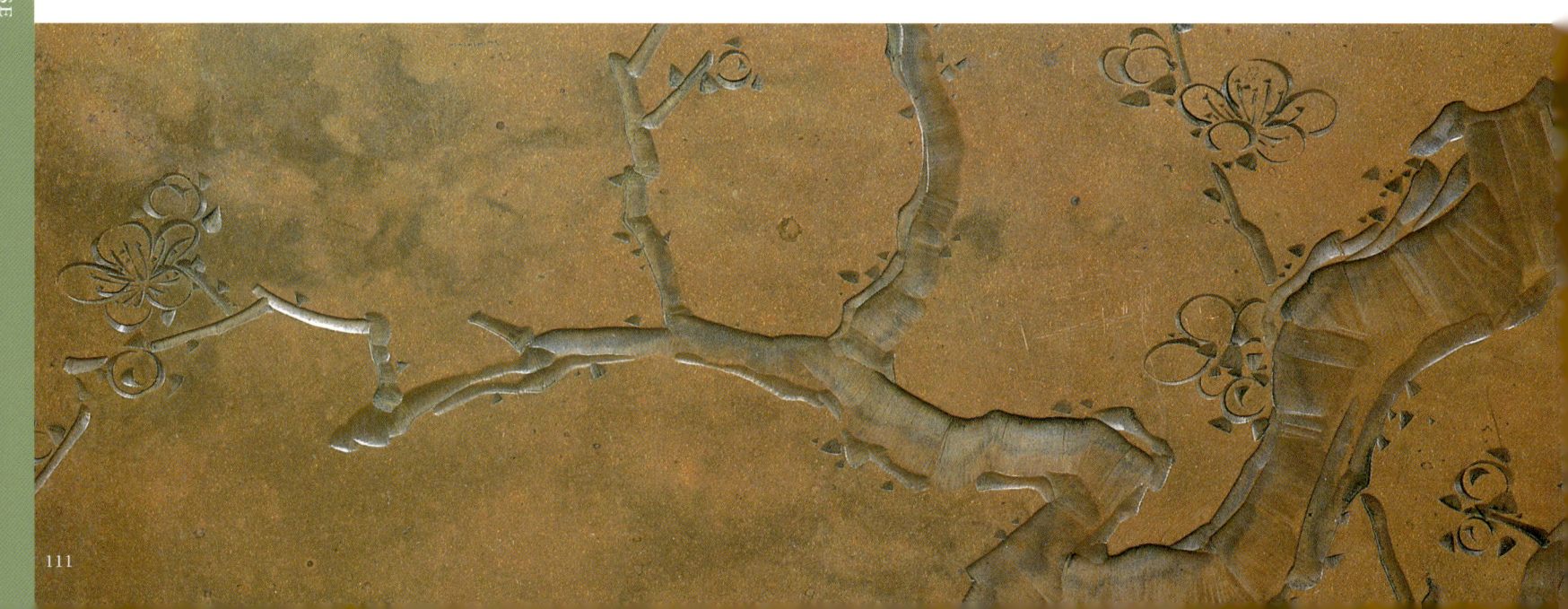

鶴ニ浪手板
真鍮地
金・銀・赤銅象嵌高彫
刻銘「勝珉」花押
九・一×一二・二
金工　三九一

魚狗手板
四分一地
銅・赤銅・金・銀・黒四分一
象嵌高彫　片切彫
刻銘「勝珉」
九・一×一二・五
金工　三九二

雀手板
四分一地
銅・赤銅・金象嵌高彫
片切彫
刻銘「六十九翁　勝珉」
九・一×一二・一
金工　三九三

112

児犬手板

真鍮地　銀・四分一・銅
赤銅象嵌高彫
片切彫
九・〇×一二・一
刻銘「芳洲叟　勝珉」
金工　三九四

牡丹手板

赤銅地
金・銀・四分一象嵌高彫
色絵
刻銘「帝室技藝員　従五位海野勝珉」
九・〇×一二・二
金工　三九五

錦魚手板

銅地　薄肉打出　金象嵌
九・〇×一二・二
刻銘「六十九翁　勝珉」
金工　三九九

鷺手板

鉄地
金・銀・四分一象嵌高彫
金・銀色絵
一二・三×九・一
刻　花押
金工　三九六

布袋片切彫手板

四分一地　薄肉打出
金・銀象嵌　片切彫
一二・二×九・一
刻銘「東京美術学校教授　海野勝珉」
金工　三九七

手板・煙草入

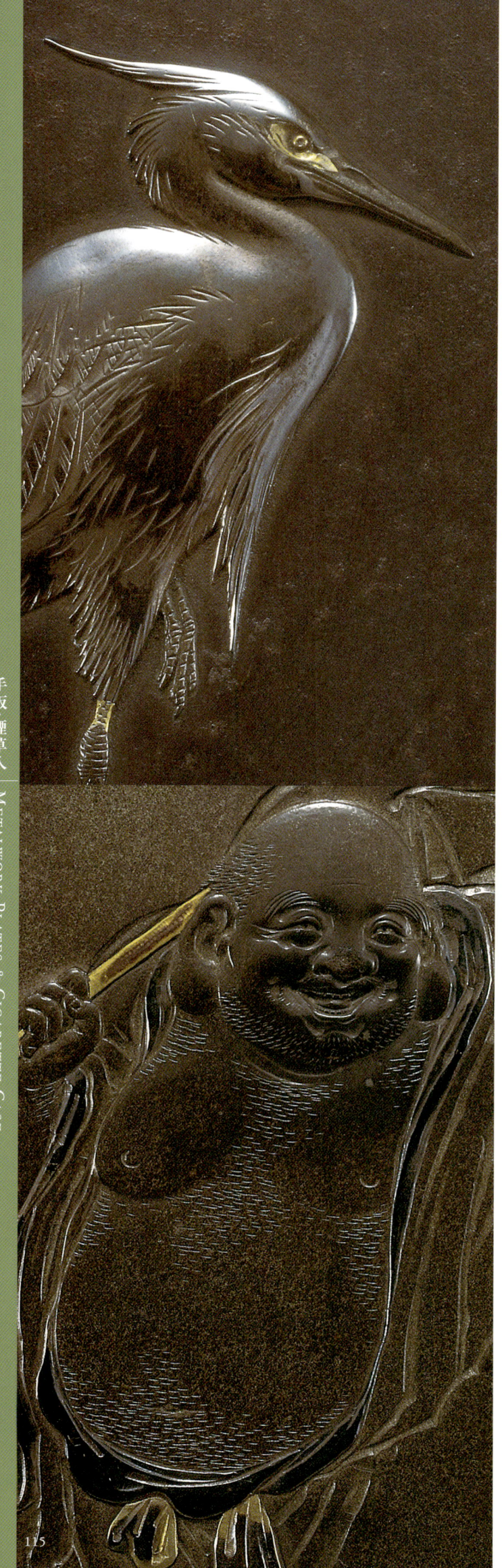

METALWORK PLATES & CIGARETTE CASE

山水片切彫手板
四分一　薄肉打出　片切彫
一二・三×九・一
刻　花押
金工　三九八

鮎手板

銀地
四分一・銅・赤銅・金・真鍮象嵌高彫
片切彫
九・〇五×一二・二
刻銘「壬子之春　芳洲辻勝珉」
金工　四〇一

秋草手板
銅地
金・銀・四分一象嵌高彫
片切彫　金色絵
九・〇×一二・二
刻銘「勝珉」
金工　四〇〇

イソップ物語図手板
四分一地
赤銅・金・銀象嵌
片切彫
裏面に羽根の図金象嵌法を示す
九・〇×一二・〇
刻銘「七十叟　勝珉」花押
金工　一六四一

肉合彫松手板

銅地　赤銅象嵌　金色絵
六・〇×九・一
刻銘「第九肉合彫松」
金工　二八八

肉彫竹手板

真鍮地
四分一・銀象嵌高彫
六・〇×九・〇五
刻銘「第十肉彫竹」
金工　二八九

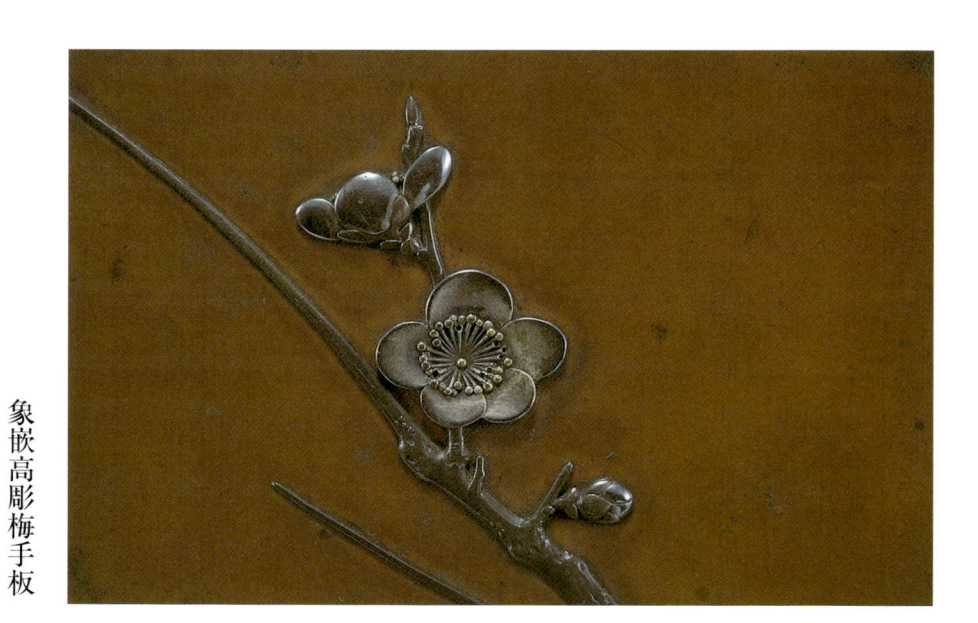

象嵌高彫梅手板

銅地
銀・四分一象嵌高彫
六・〇×九・一
刻銘「第十一象嵌高彫梅」
金工　二九〇

118

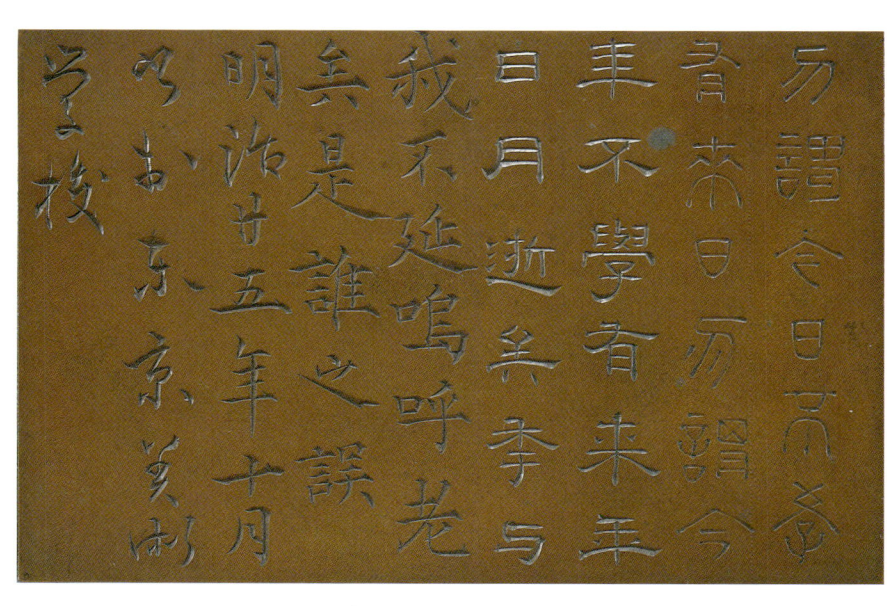

文字彫刻法手板

銅地　毛彫　片切彫
六〇・〇×九〇・〇
刻銘「第四文字彫刻法
教授今泉雄作書
助教授海野勝珉刻」
金工　二九五

柳馬図巻煙草入

銅地
赤銅・四分一・金・銀象嵌
片切彫
一三・〇×七・五
刻銘「勝珉」金象嵌印「芳洲生」
金工 二四九

拓本

拓本は彫金の鏨の巧妙な線や浮き彫りの凹凸をうつしとって実際に制作された作品の記録として多数つくられた。写真や図案では伝わらない細やかな技の冴えを示し、それこそが海野勝珉の作品の魅力の一つである。「海野家資料」には海野勝珉、珉乗、秀珉の作品だけでなく、弟子や江戸時代の彫金家の作品の拓本が含まれ、この時代の彫金研究にとっても興味深い資料である。

Rubbings

A large number of rubbings were made transferring the skillful lines of the chisel and uneven relief on to paper, recording the surfaces of completed works. They show the intricate skill that is one of the main features of Unno's work, that cannot be shown in photographs or designs. The Unno Family Material includes rubbings of not only work by Unno Shomin, Minjo and Shumin, but also works of metal carving artists of the Edo period and pupils, making it interesting material for research of this area.

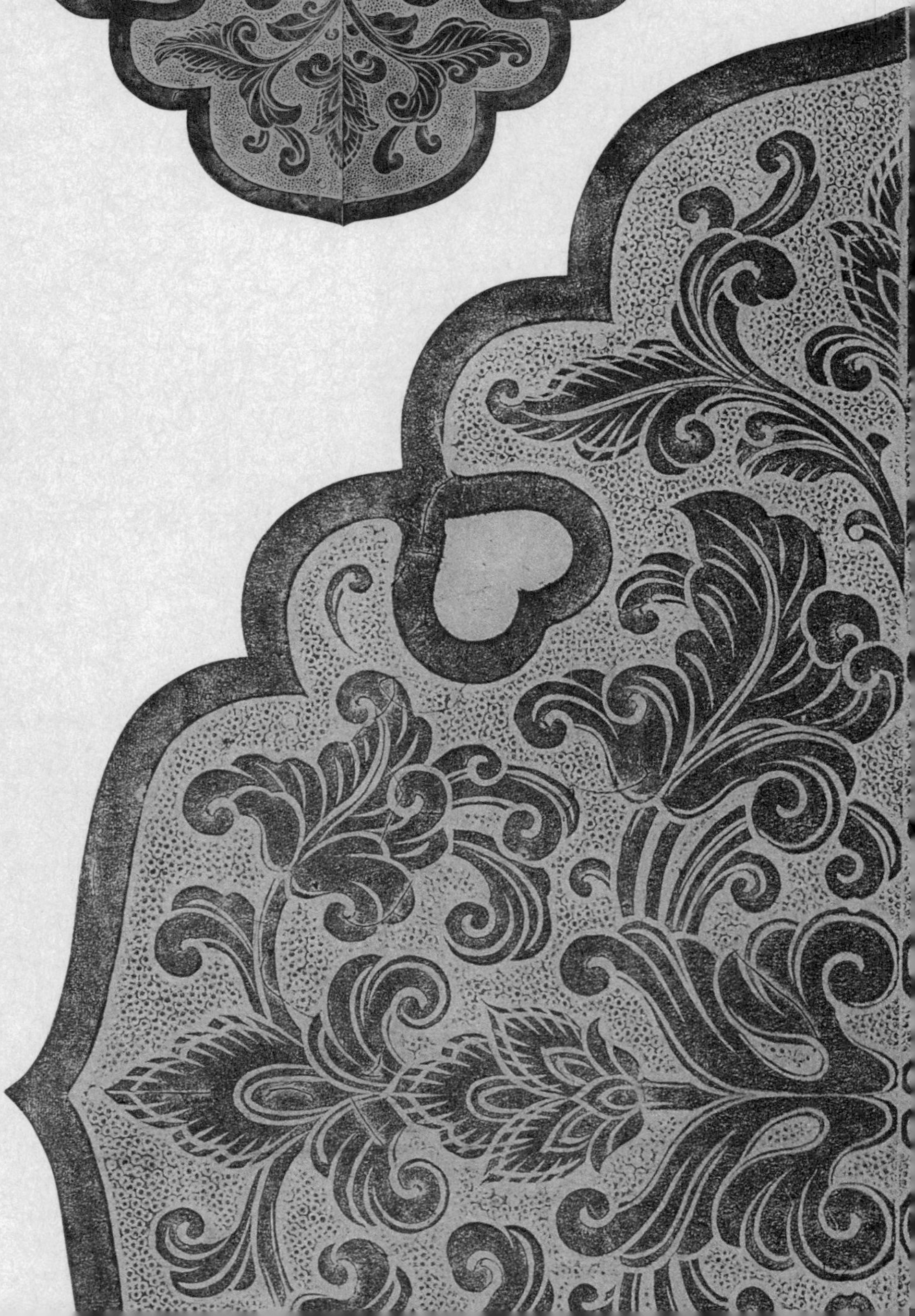

拓本 RUBBINGS

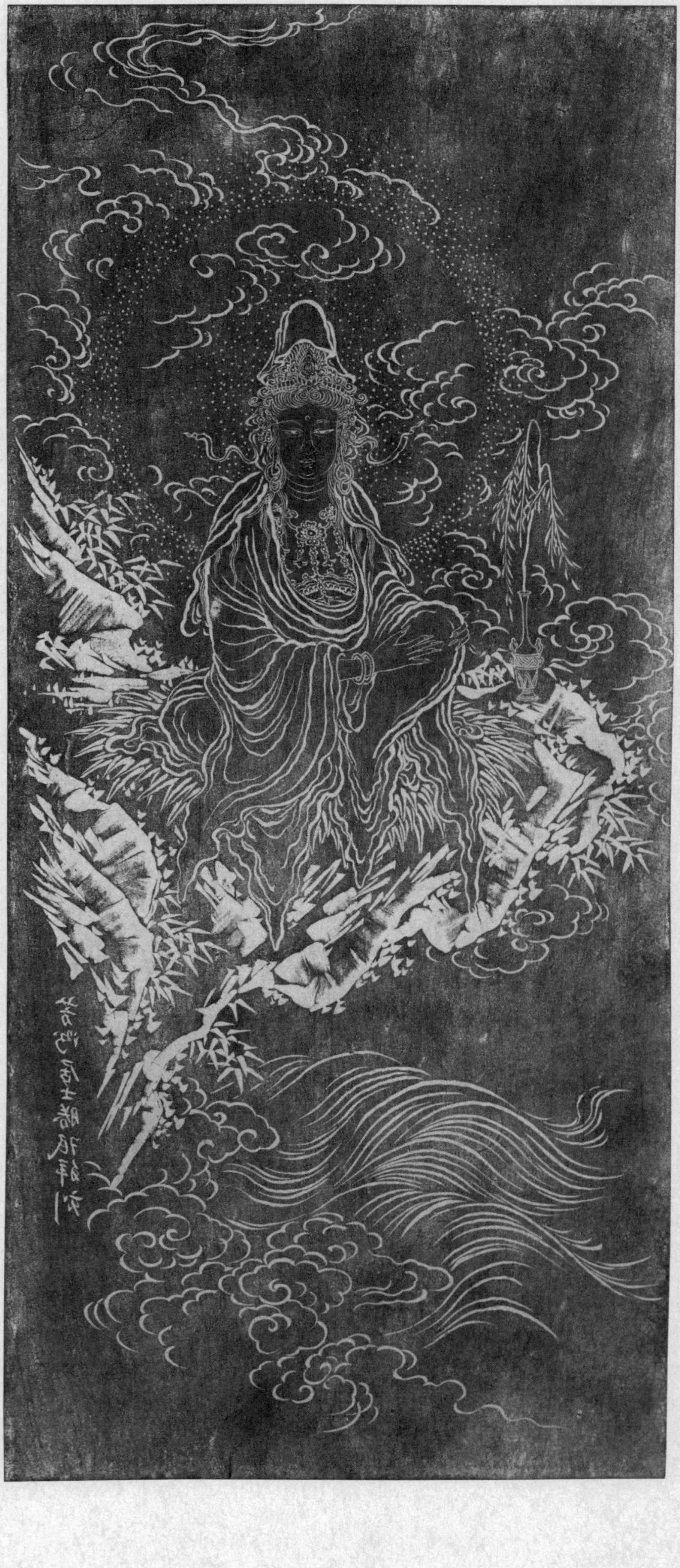

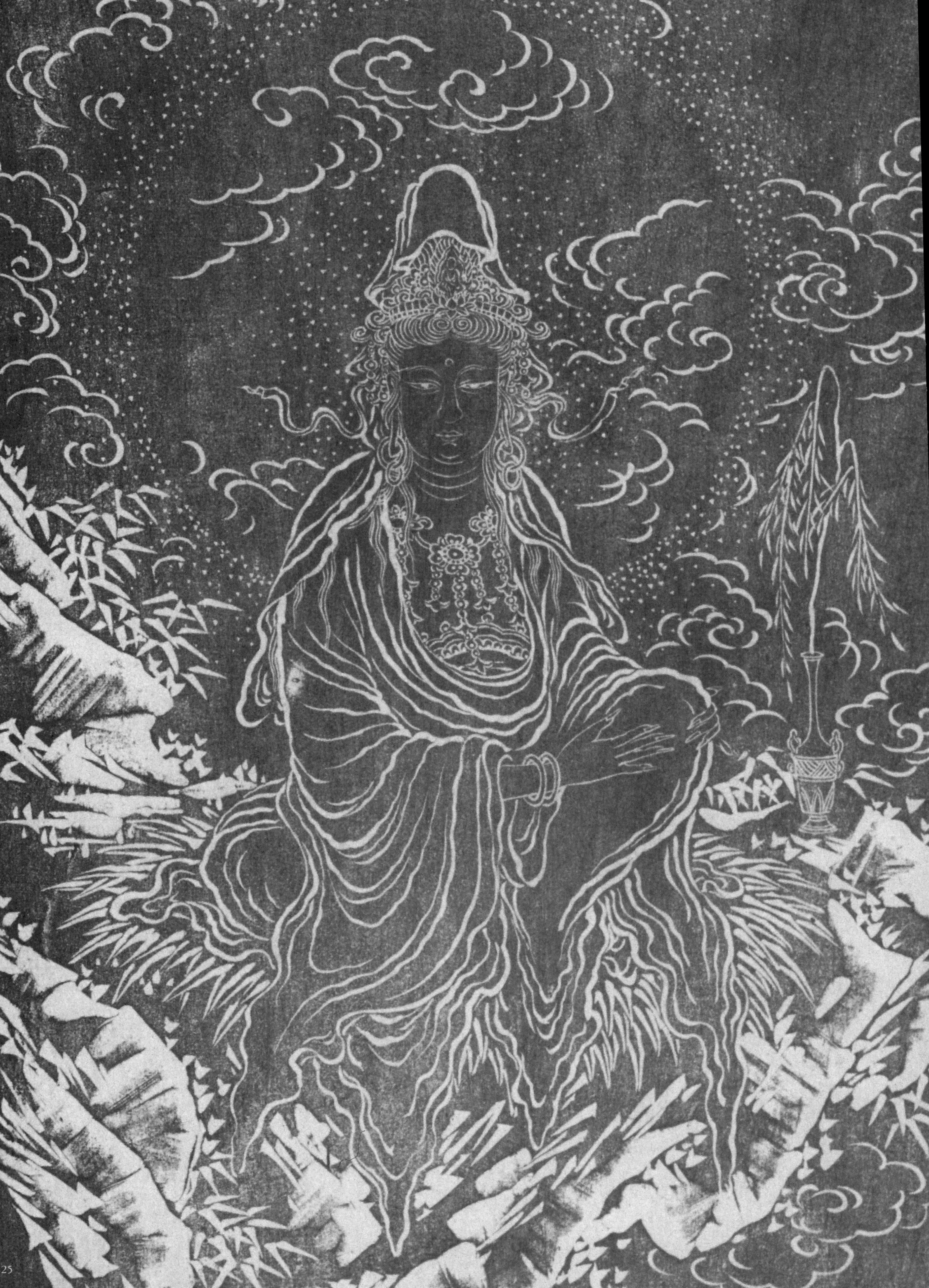

126

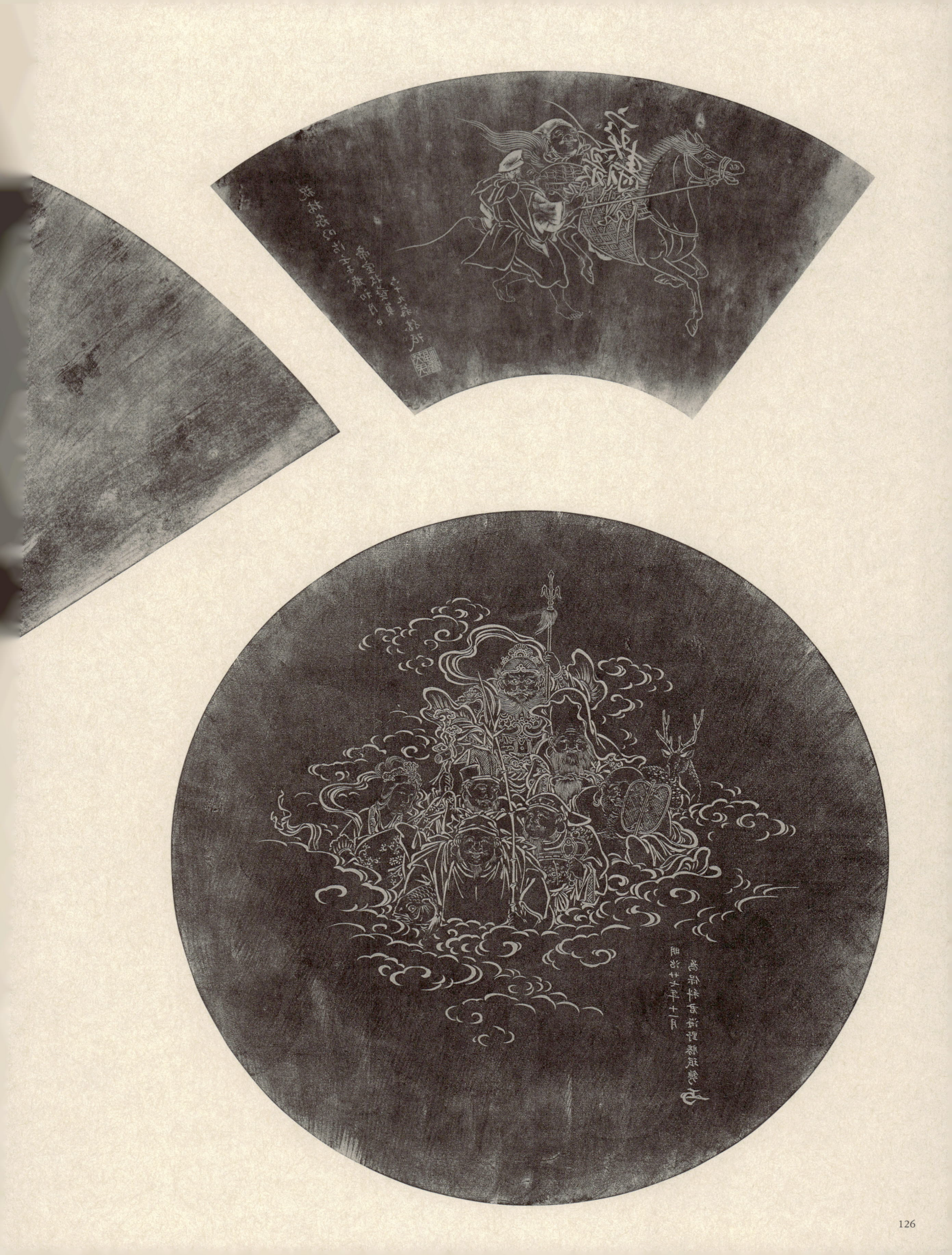

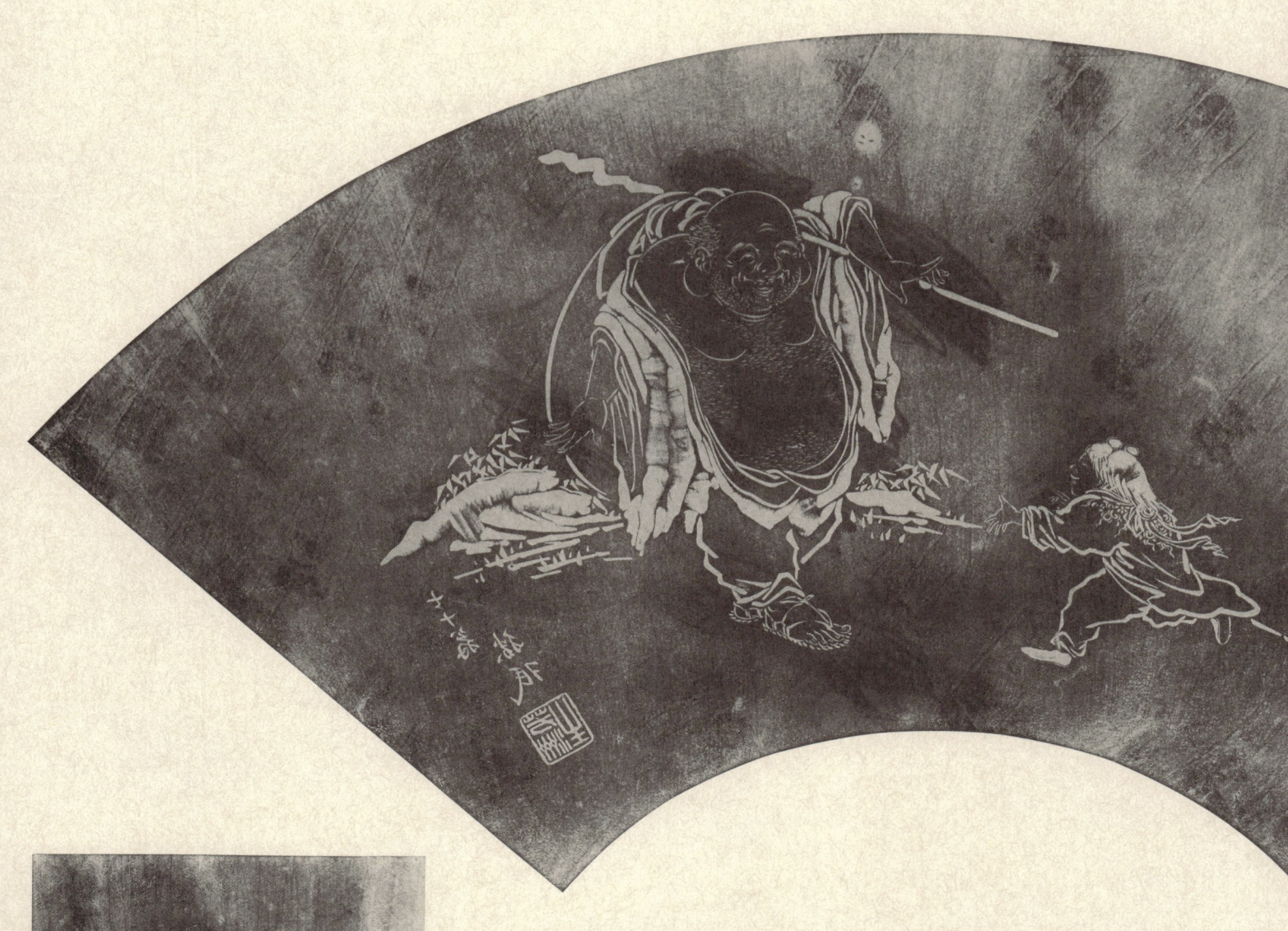

拓本 | RUBBINGS

128

拓本 | RUBBINGS

130

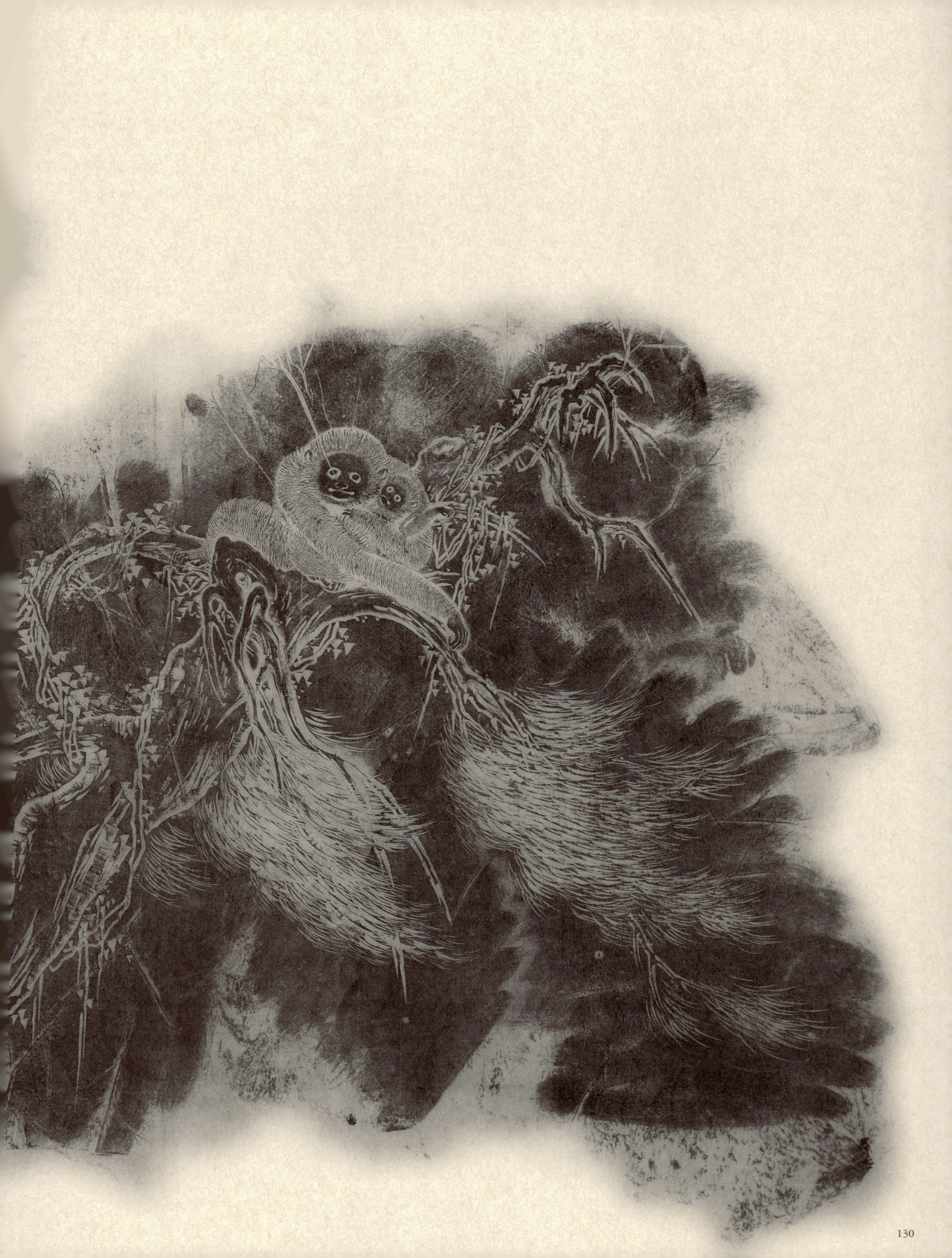

拓本｜RUBBINGS

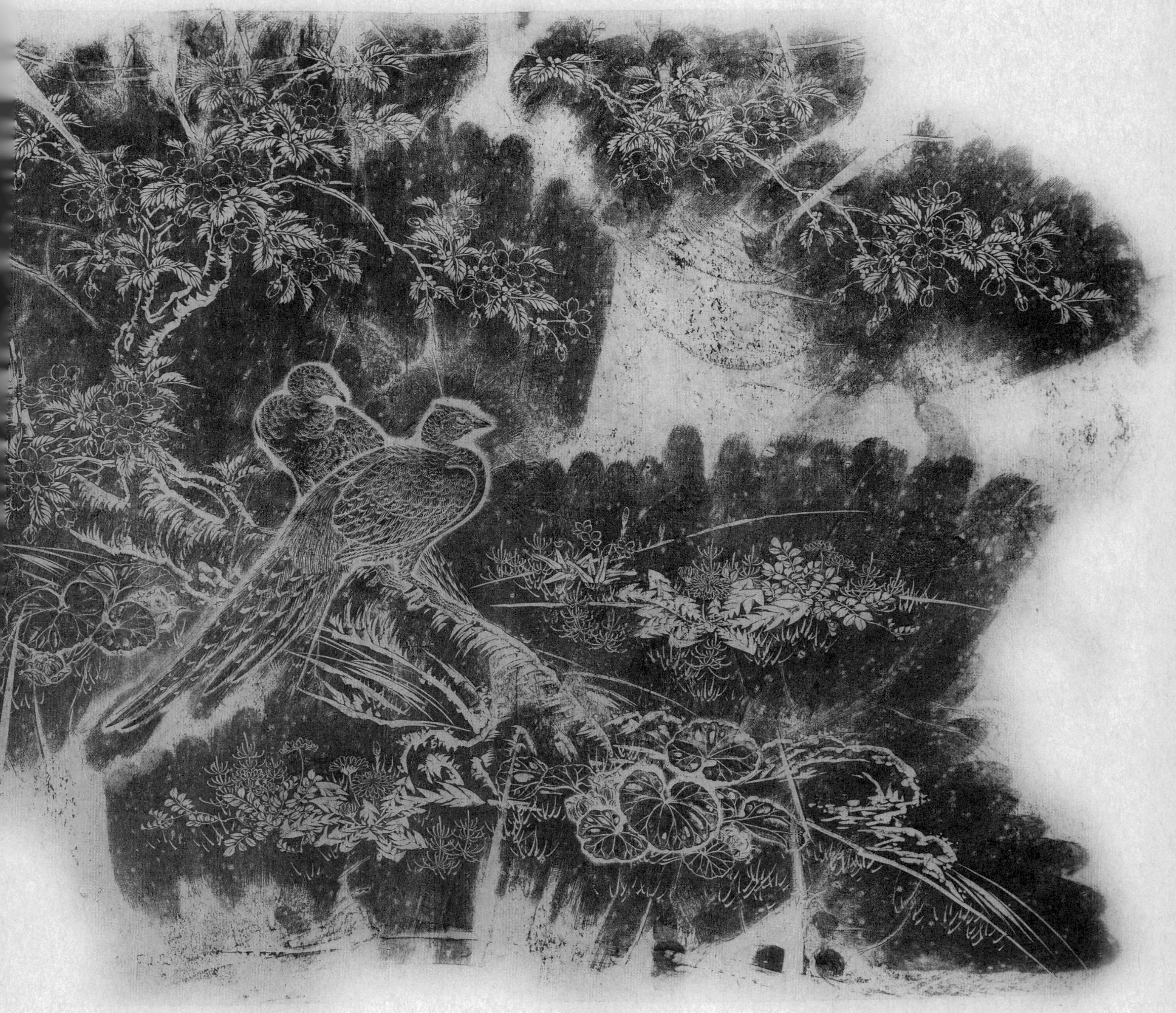

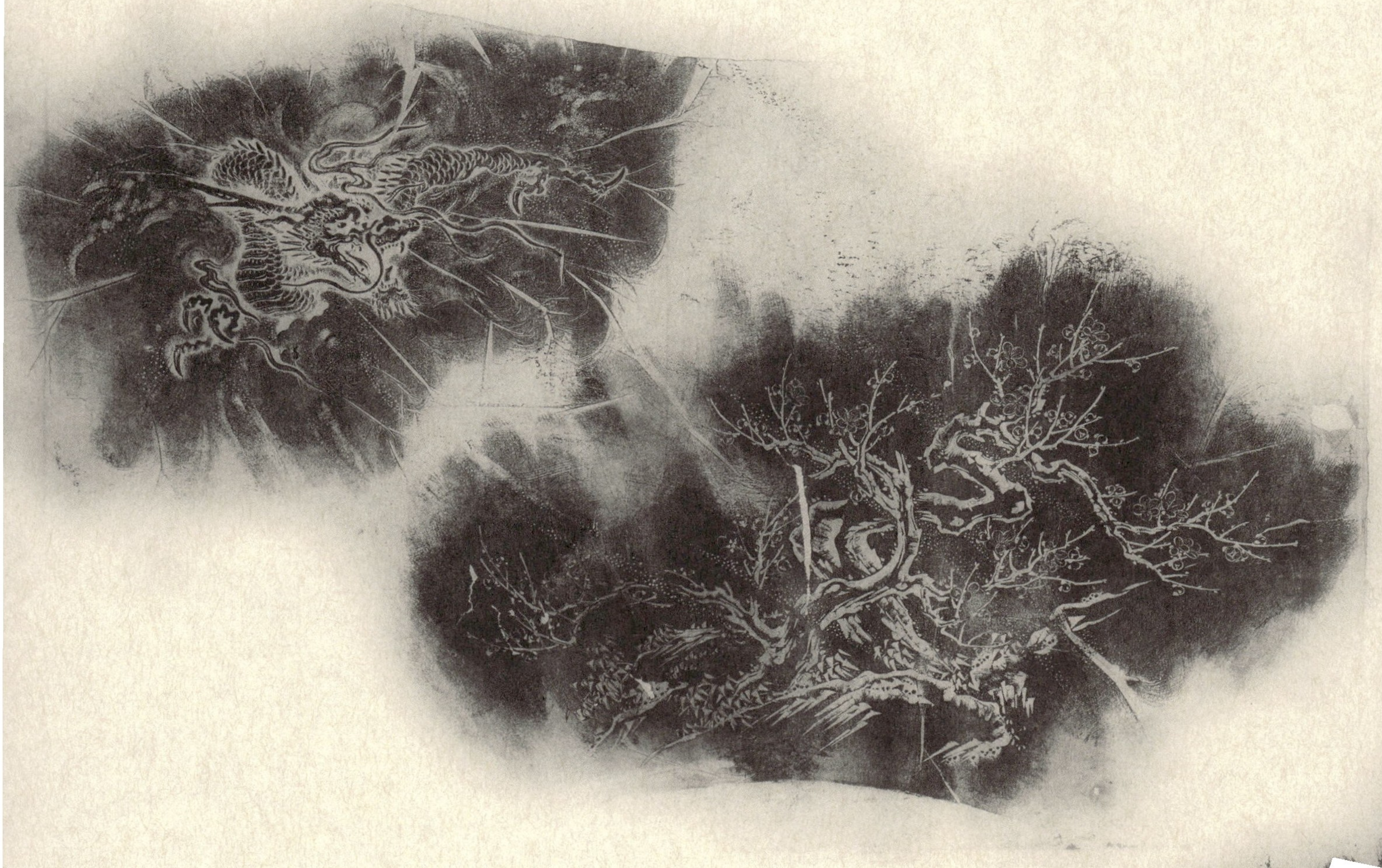

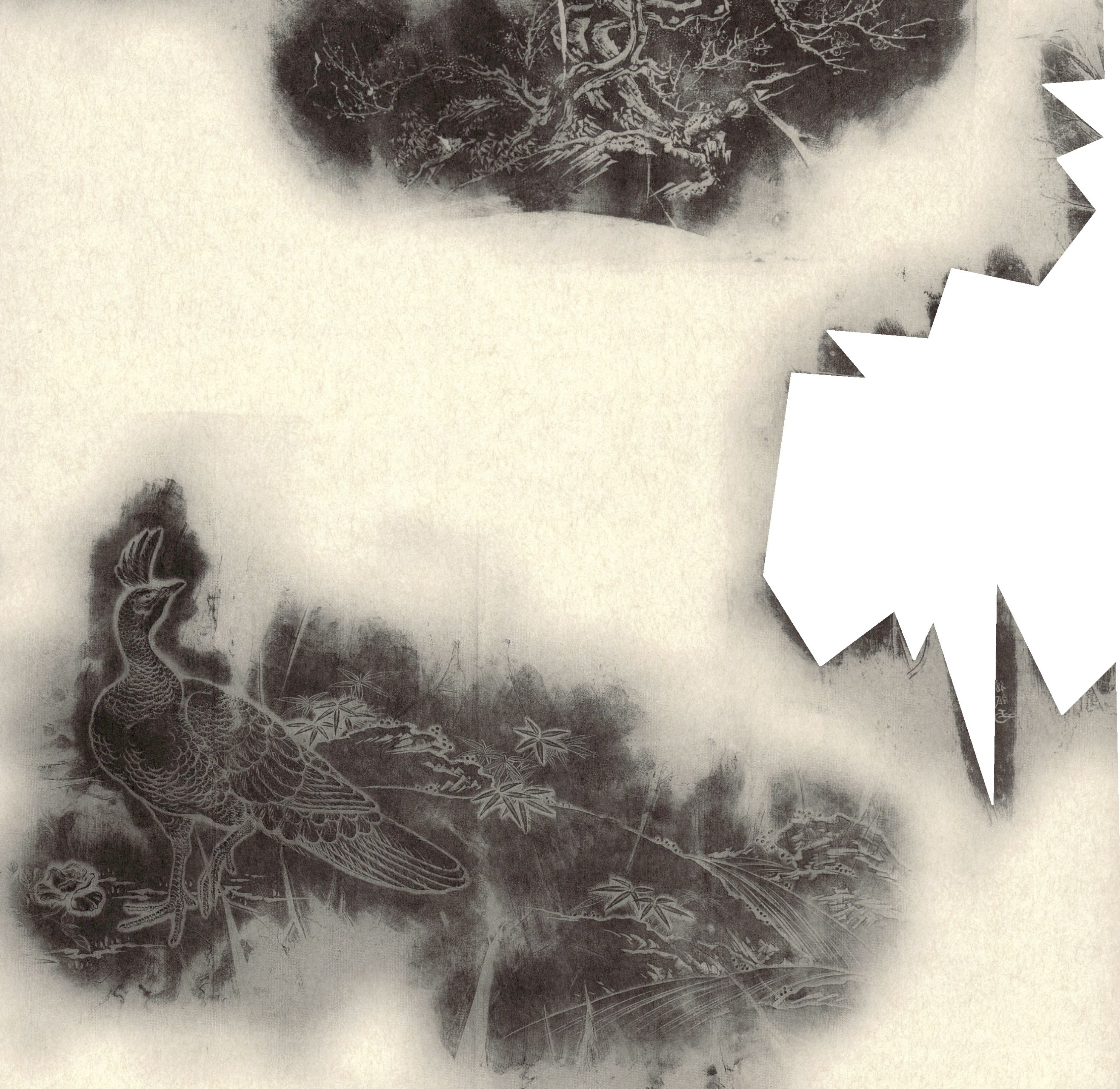

134

拓本　RUBBINGS

136

海野勝珉関係資料について　横溝廣子

海野勝珉賞状一覧

海野勝珉関係資料について

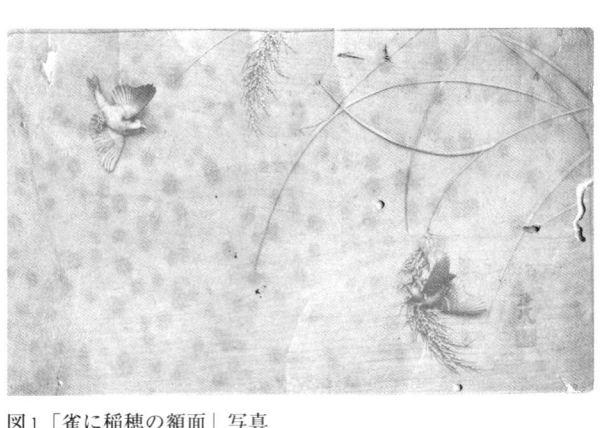

横溝廣子

近代日本の彫金界を代表する一人である海野勝珉は東京芸術大学美術学部の前身である東京美術学校の彫金教育を、その草創期による明治時代を通じて担った唯一の教官であった。また、長男の豊太郎（珉乗）、三男の銀三郎（盛乗）と四男の清（秀珉）も東京美術学校で彫金を学び、清もまた美術学校および東京芸術大学の彫金教授として長年つとめた。この東京芸術大学との深い縁により、海野家に伝わった下絵、写生、拓本などの資料が昭和四十五（一九七〇）年にご遺族から当大学に寄贈され、《海野家資料》（註1）と題して現在までにごく一部が紹介・公開されてきた。海野家の作品だけでなく、江戸時代や同時代のほかの彫金家の図案や拓本、また同時代の画家、図案家の図も含む多岐にわたる資料であるが、できるだけそのエッセンスを抽出した海野勝珉に関係する資料を選択して本書の図版に掲載した。本稿ではその中のいくつかの今まで海野勝珉との関連であまり触れられることがなかった資料について紹介するが、まずは読者の便宜のために海野勝珉について述べることから始めたい。

海野勝珉の略歴

海野勝珉の略歴を示すにあたって、調べた資料（註2）がそれぞれに微妙な違いがあり、ここではできる限りこれらをまとめることを試みる。（なお、作品については、本稿の最後に付す賞状一覧に含まれているものは記載していない。）

天保十五（一八四四）年五月十五日常陸国水戸下市肴町に海野伝右衛門の四男として生まれる。名は竹次郎。嘉永五（一八五二）年に九歳で叔父水戸藩士海野美三郎（初代美盛）に就き金属彫刻を四年間学んだ後、十三歳で水戸藩士萩谷勝平（通称、彌兵衛）の五番目の弟子としての呼称である彌五郎と呼ばれる。この間に漢籍を武庄次郎に学び、絵画を足立梅渓に学び、また、水戸藩お抱えの鎚金師明珍義臣に師事し、鍛金技法を身につける。また、幼少のころから常磐津、踊、三味線などの稽古で非凡の才能をしめし、後の雅楽をモチーフとする作品の究極の表現につながる。

慶応三（一八六七）年頃、二十四歳で水戸で開業し、萩谷勝平の一字をもらって基平と号する。明治四（一八七一）年頃、東京に出て（明治元年などとする文献もある）勝珉より五歳上で駒込村で彫金を営んでいた兄の真田幸次郎（静國）のところに寓居し、ともに若松屋の袋物金具を製造する。この頃から萩谷勝平の一字と横谷宗珉を意識したといわれる勝珉と名乗る。明治六年、小石川区指ヶ谷町の雁金守親に師事して、花鳥の彫技を学び、家具装飾・携帯品の彫金技術をみがく。明治九年に千駄木町に業を開き、同年の廃刀例で刀装具の製作をあきらめ、花瓶、香炉、置物、烟草入金具、巻烟草入、香函、緒締、指輪の制作に従事する。明治十年第一回内国勧業博覧会に刀装具の技術をそのまま生かした《神代人物金製袋物錠》を出品し、褒状を受賞する。この頃の業名は東花斎勝珉を用いている。明治十四年第二回内国勧業博覧会に《雀に稲穂の額面》（50頁参照、図1）などを出品、褒状受賞。この写真を確認する限り、雀は刀装具の高彫をはるかに上回る打ち出しの立体的な表現による作品である。明治二十年頃、ウィリアム・スタージ

図1「雀に稲穂の額面」写真
fig.1 Photograph of "Sparrow and ear of rice"

ス・ビゲロウの依頼により、狩野芳崖下図の《鬼の宝鈴を曳く図》（図3）の銀製胸飾を制作し、フェノロサや岡倉天心にその技量をみとめられる。明治二十年春より、雅楽の伶人辻高節に舞楽蘭陵王の装束、態度に関する懇切丁密な指導を受けた後、《蘭陵王置物》の制作にかかる。明治二十一年、東京彫工会の人選により皇后陛下宝冠勲章の彫刻を御前彫刻する。明治二十二年、天皇陛下日本美術協会行幸の際、銀製コップを御前彫刻する。この年に東京彫工会第四回競技会審査員依嘱せられ、以後同会および日本美術協会の審査員、役員をたびたび嘱託される（以後、主な審査員などの役職としては明治二十三年第三回内国勧業博覧会品評人、明治二十八年第四回内国勧業博覧会審査員、明治三十六年第五回内国勧業博覧会審査官、明治四十年東京勧業博覧会審査官、大正三（一九一三）年第一回農商務省図案及応用作品展覧会審査委員、大正五年東京大正博覧会審査官および第二回農商務省図案及応用作品展覧会審査委員）。

明治二十三年第三回内国勧業博覧会にて代表作《蘭陵王置物》（宮内庁三の丸尚蔵館所蔵）を出品、妙技一等賞受賞。同年七月二日東京美術学校雇を命ぜられ、七月二十七日に東京美術学校初代彫金教授加納夏雄と師弟の誓義を結ぶ。ここにおいて加納夏雄とともに、はじめて学校の中での彫金教育の基礎をつくり、その実践に当たる。明治二十四年には東京美術学校助教授に任ぜられる。明治二十六年、シカゴ・コロンブス万博に再び雅楽をモチーフとする《還城楽図額》（東京国立博物館所蔵、72頁参照）を、当時の博覧会事務局による絵画の形状にし示スヲ主トシタルモノ」にする方針に従って額装された絵画の形状にして出品し、銅牌特別賞状を受ける。明治二十七年逓信省官吏依託純銀花瓶製作主任に任命され、同年東京美術学校教授を勤める。明治二十九年帝室技芸員に任命、東京美術学校彫金教授に昇任する。（三十一年から三十七年まで彫金兼鍛金の教授）。明治三十二年、三井家の注文により《桐鳳凰文銀装兵庫鎖太刀拵》を手がける（大正三年五月完成）。明治三十三年の巴里万国博覧会に《太平楽置物》（宮内庁三の丸尚蔵館所蔵）などを出品する。明治三十五年東京美術学校彫金科主任に任命される。明治三十六年日本美術協会特別会員、翌三十七年に東京彫工会終身会員となる。明治三十八年第三十七回日本美術協会美術展覧会に《銀製四季花鳥象眼高彫花瓶》（16頁参照）出品、金牌をうける。明治四十三年皇后陛下第二十五回彫工競技会行啓の際、銀製色紙へ歌を御前彫刻する。同年日英博覧会に《紅蘿小禽》（銀地象嵌花盛器）》出品、名誉賞受賞、《寒山拾得《銀彫花瓶》》《錦鶏　銀四分一小函》などを出品する。大正四年十月八日歿、七十二才。特旨により叙従四位、叙勲四等授瑞宝章。

上記において、少し補足させていただきたい。多くの新聞報道などのもととなったと思われる明治二十九年に勝珉が帝室技芸員に推薦される時の推薦文を紹介すると、

東京府東京市本郷区駒込東片町百五十二番戸

平民金彫工海野勝珉

弘化元年五月十五日生

常陸國水戸ノ人長シテ水戸藩士海野美盛ニ就キ金彫術ヲ学フコト四年后チ同藩士萩谷勝平ニ師事シ十有一年ニシテ卒業ス明治元年出京開業シ同六年小石川住雁金守親ニ就キ花鳥ノ彫技ヲ習ヒ同十年内国勧業博覧會ニ出品シテ褒状ヲ賜ヒタル廿一年以後美術展覧會及彫工競技會等ニ銅牌銀牌ノ賞ヲ受ケ廿三年第三回内国勧業博覧會ニ八素銅象眼彫蘭陵王置物ニ對シ妙技一等賞ヲ賜リ名聲頓ニ加ハリ彫技最モ上達セリ其四月該會品評人トナリ七月東京美術学校雇トナリ其年加納夏雄ノ随テ片切彫等ノ技ヲ傳フ廿四年八月同校助教授ニ任シ廿七年十一月教授ニ進ミ從七位ニ叙セラル廿八年第四囘博覧會ニ第一部第二部ノ審査官トナリ其出品及製造人トシテ有功ニ二等妙技二等ノ賞牌ヲ賜ハリ而シテ製品時ニ長短ナキ能ハストハ雖トモ其技ニ誇リ他ヲ侮ルカ如キ自負心ナキ彼レカ如キハ蓋シ希ナリ《帝室技芸員予薦》東京国立博物館史資料216（マイクロフィルム番号M2335）

これに対して明治十二年に刊行された『東京名工鑑』（東京府勧業課）においては、「初メ常州ニ於テ萩谷勝平ニ就キ十三歳ヨリ十一ヶ年間修

業シ廿四歳ノ時同地ニ開業シ明治五年ニ出京兄静國方へ寓居営業シ若松屋ノ嘱品袋物金具ヲ製造シ今ヨリ二ケ年前當所ニ轉居シ以來追々景況宜シ」と記載しており、千駄木開業から二、三年しか経っていない時点で公刊された最もはやい記録であり、東京に出た年を明治五年としている。また、桑原洋次郎『日本装剣金工史』では、桑原氏が勝珉から直接送られたという略伝には「海野勝珉 幼名竹次郎、又彌五郎、藻税軒基平又貞月庵・明治四年東京に出で勝珉と改称す。東華斎又芳洲といふ」とあることから、水戸での開業が慶応三年から翌明治元年年頃で、東京に出たのが明治四、五年頃とする方を採用した。ちなみに、東京美術学校における教官履歴書には萩谷勝平、武庄次郎、足立梅渓に学んだという記述の次に明治九年に東京駒込千駄木町に開業した、としか記されていない。

それはさておき、上記の帝室技芸員の推薦文の最後の「其技ニ誇リ他ヲ侮ルカ如キ自負心ナキ」は希なことである、と結んでいる点が彼への評価として何を意味するのであろうか。勝珉の死去を伝える読売新聞の大正四年十月九日朝刊の記事に「資性温厚世俗に関せず、純芸術家気質を有し嘗て他の技術を罵れることなし」と特筆している点から見ても、このことを強調した人がまわりにいた。

勝珉についての文献ではあまり触れられることがないが、錬鉄の名工といわれた水戸藩お抱えの鎚金師の明珍紀義臣が甲冑の制作に従事していたころに勝珉が師事し、その訓育の影響を強く受けたということから、鍛金のうちの鎚金技法をも身につけていたという(船越春秀『日本の彫金』三彩社、昭和四十九年)。さらに東京美術学校において鍛金科が設置された翌年の「東京美術学校一覧 従明治廿九年 至明治三十年」における次の彫金科と鍛金科の教員名簿によれば、教授は海野勝珉であった(註3)。

「美術工藝科

　彫金科

　教授　　帝室技藝員　加納夏雄

　助教授　向井繁太郎

　全　　　　　　　岡部覺彌

　鍛金科

　教授　兼彫金　帝室技藝員　海野勝珉

　全　　　　　　　　　桜井正次

　嘱託教員　平田惣之助」

以後「東京美術学校一覧」によれば明治三十七年まで、海野勝珉は彫金兼鍛金の教授と記される。そして明治三十八年には、彫金科と鍛金科は金工科として統合される。(なお設置時は教授をおかず、その年だけ鍛金兼彫金の助教授として向井繁太郎が記載されたが、その後は彫金のみであった。)

鍛金科設置の時にその教育に当ったのは平田惣之助(明治四十年に宗幸と改名)と桜井正次であるが、桜井正次は三十一年に辞職、平田はいったん明治三十年八月に辞め、再び三十一年五月から嘱託のままの雇用であった。大正六年に帝室技芸員に任命されてからようやく翌年東京美術学校の雇用が嘱託から教授になった。鍛金家が彫金家は仕上げの鏨仕事を担当するのみということが通例であり、実際にそのような仕事の分担で制作されている海野勝珉を含む同時代の彫金家の作品は数多い。ここで次のような《蘭陵王置物》における鍛金の技の評判に注目したい。「氏が其刀を起こさんとするや先づ鍛金法に則り所」「人物彫像を作り着々其基礎を定む是れ氏が尋常彫金家と技倆を異にせる所」「人物彫像に鋳工の手を假らずして全形を鎚出し而も其眞を失なはざるが如き眞に空前の精作と稱すべしとて識者皆其妙技に感ぜざるなかりき。」(読売新聞、明治二十九年八月三日「素銅彫蘭陵王の置物」)(註4)

金属を用いた造形を行なった職種の間には明確な分類がなされ、その間に意識および地位の差がある時代であった。このことがわかりやすく次の新聞記事に記載されている。「古来彫金の術は、みな鏨工の専門に蹈して、鍛鋳の両技と交えず。たまたまこれを兼ねれば、乱雑の賤工を以て目せられ、家彫もしくは腰元の陳套は彫金家と呼ばるるもの、終に脱することを能はざりし所なりき。鎚鍛の技は、半肉以上の彫鏤に、その少分を用ひざることを得ざりしも、それを以てその大部分を、外に置くべからざりしも、鍛工として卑しめられたり。これを以て、勝珉氏が陵王を成す時は、全く彫金の範囲外に置くべからざりしも、また鍛工たる彫工の嚆矢として、彼の方寸以内の小品に蹈踏したりし用ひたる彫金製作の嚆矢として、世の彫工の眼を覚ましつ。」(読売新聞、明治二十九年五月十一日「月曜

付録　桜丘偶話」）

つまり《蘭陵王置物》において、技法による地位の格差に対する偏見の壁のある中で「他の技術を罵れることな」く、卑しまれる可能性のある鍛金を多く用いた作品を発表するのは「世の彫工の眼を覚ま」す画期的なことであった。これが海野勝珉の偉大な業績とみなすべきであろう。これを湛えるかのように東京美術学校は海野勝珉の死亡を伝える記事に本人の写真とともに、《蘭陵王置物》の写真を大きく掲載したのである（図2）。

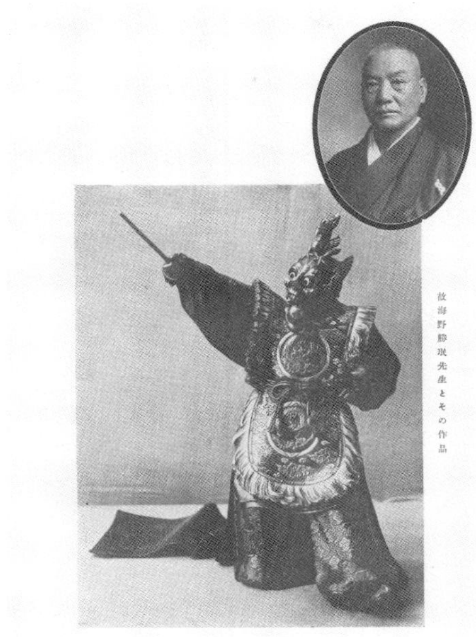

図2「故海野勝珉先生とその作品」
『東京美術学校校友会月報』第14巻第6号
（大正4年11月30日）死亡記事より転載
fig.2 “Unno Shomin and his work”, from the obituary in Tokyo Bijutsu Gakko Koyukai Geppo

海野家資料

海野勝珉の業績を通覧したところで、本題である彼とその一族が残した数々の制作に関わる資料の内容についていくつか図案に焦点をあてながら紹介したい。

《海野家資料》は巻子装下図八巻、画帖装写生下絵二十一冊、画帖装拓本二十三冊と二帖、賞状綴込帳三冊（勝珉二冊、珉乗一冊）および多数の模本類からなる。これらの資料から海野勝珉がどういう画家や彫金家の作品を研究、参照し、多数の作品を制作したかがわかる。その旺盛な意欲は例えば次の記事の言葉からも想像することができる。

「翁は他の美術家が一風變わって美術界の名譽職を厭ふに反して己が相當におもへばどんな、會の役員でも勤める又出品といへばどこへでも間に合さへすれば出品する、而してこの出品も役員も自分の虚榮心の為でない事は、既にあれ丈の榮譽を持って居られるのでも分る、唯これは斯うせねば會の為に悪かろう、後進の奬勵にもなるまいとの赤心から出るので、つまり平民主義の發露に他ならぬ」（「海野勝珉翁」書画骨董雑誌第二十四号、明治四十三年五月）。

巻子も画帖も内容的に明確な分類ができないものが多いが、強いていえば下記の内訳で示すとおりである。（なお、本書掲載図が下記のうちのどの資料に収録されているかは150頁に示す。）

写生下絵1（画帖）「下繪張込」三三・〇×四〇・五（花瓶や置物）
写生下絵2（画帖）「動物写生□之諸鳥類」三三・〇×四〇・五（鳥類）
写生下絵3（画帖）二三・八×三一・五（魚や昆虫）
写生下絵4（画帖）「下繪帖」二七・二×一九・三（香炉、煙草入、皿など）
写生下絵5（画帖）「下繪帖」二七・二×一九・四（煙草入、皿）
写生下絵6（画帖）「下繪帖」二七・二×一九・三（煙草入、鳥、動物）
写生下絵7（画帖）二七・二×一九・四（植物）
写生下絵8（画帖）「彫金画稿　壹」二七・二×一九・三
写生下絵9（画帖）「彫金画稿　二」二七・二×一九・三
写生下絵10（画帖）「彫金画稿　三」二七・二×一九・三
写生下絵11（画帖）「彫金画稿　四」二七・一×一九・二（鍔、拓本）
写生下絵12（画帖）「彫金画稿　五」二七・一×一九・二
写生下絵13（画帖）「天保年間春英下繪并二諸名家筆」「小道具下繪本」一七・〇×二四・四（刀装具）
写生下絵14（画帖）「天保年間春英下繪并二諸名家筆」「小道具下繪本」一七・〇×二四・四（刀装具）
写生下絵15（画帖）「明治三十九年より四十年三月迄下繪」二二・五×一五・八（花瓶）
写生下絵16（画帖）「切図拾遺」一五・〇×二二・〇
写生下絵17（画帖）「切図拾遺」一五・〇×二二・〇
写生下絵18（画帖）「切図拾遺」一五・〇×二二・〇
写生下絵19（画帖）三二・〇×二三・五（植物や鳥類）
写生下絵20（画帖）三二・〇×二三・五（動物や鳥類、魚、昆虫）
写生下絵21（画帖）三二・〇×二三・五（神仏、仙人、人物など）
巻子下図1　三七・五×一七九三・七「花鳥山水　花瓶下絵」二十七図
巻子下図2　三七・五×一五七六・〇「宮内省花瓶下絵」三十四図
巻子下図3　四四・〇×九〇九・八「花瓶下繪」十八図
巻子下図4　四七・六×九四〇・六「勧業銀行　銀花瓶下絵」十二図
巻子下図5　五〇・二×七一四・六「山水花瓶下絵」九図
巻子下図6　五〇・七×二七四・〇「蔦　下繪」

図3　狩野芳崖下図の「鬼の宝鈴を曳く図」
fig.3　Kano Hogai, Design for a Clasp
Ink and gold on silk, Image 21.2×33.7cm, overall 59.5×52.6cm
Museum of Fine Arts Boston, William Sturgis Bigelow Collection
Photograph©2006 Museum of Fine Arts, Boston

巻子下図

巻子下図　画面七七・三×七五・〇「反魂香」(漢の武帝と李夫人の故事　83頁参照)

画面五三・五×六五・七　福地復一考案「網引図」(66、67頁参照)

下絵の中には、勝珉筆の図以外に「応挙」、「景文」、「探幽斎」「一蝶」などの図のうつしや印刷物、柴田是真、石川光明、長命是春、川端玉章などの名もしばしば見られる。また、拓本の中には「倣牧溪画　勝珉刻」「宮本二天意　勝珉刻」「倣応挙之図　帝室技芸員　芳洲叟勝珉刻」「牧溪画　勝珉刻」「米僊画　勝珉鑴」「和亭画　勝珉刻」、「玉章画　勝珉意　勝珉刻」「勝珉刀華邨図」の銘が見られ、美術学校手板(105～119頁参照)には「応挙意　勝珉刻」「李龍眠意勝珉刻」と銘を切っている。つまり、勝珉は画家の絵を彫金の技で表現することをよくしたことを示す。これは勝珉の感覚では、プライドをもって巧妙な技を示す手段としてさまざまな著名な画家のスタイルを用いたと解釈すべきであり、下絵について勝珉自身が記した言葉に次のことが述べられている。

「維新後廃刀令出でて、刀剣の装飾も廃り彫金を更めて他の装飾に用ふらるる様に成ってから、依頼者の鑑識も下がって、中には下絵を持ってこれに肉を付けて呉れなどとの注文さへある様に成った、前にも述べた通り、繪画には繪画の規則、彫金には彫金の掟がある、一乘でも掟にかなはるべきであるが、當時そんな事は思ひも寄らぬ、只華美を競ふ憐れな状態となった、‥‥」「桑原某の著書に、宗珉は一蝶の下圖によって工を施し、一乘の下繪はいつも容齋が描いたなどとあるけれども、實地を知らぬ言草である、第一彫金をするふのでは名人でも先生でもない、一ヶ下圖をつけて貰ふのでは名人でも先生でもない、其工合も鹽梅して下繪をかかなければとても面白いものは出来ないのは分明である」(「彫金界の氣運　帝室技藝員海野勝珉氏談」《書畫骨董雜誌》三一、明治四十四年)。この他にも「近古金工談」《日本美術》九十一号、明治三十九年九月)においても「宗珉ほどの名人でも畫が出来ないので探幽や一蝶に下書を依頼したなどといひますが此は全くの素人考へ

であります」。桑原某の著書とは桑原羊次郎著『装劍金工談』(明治三十七年)における「彫金工と下繪師」の項だと思われるが、そこでは「名工上手と稱せらるるものは、好んで時の名畫師に就き、親しく其の補助を得たりしことは、歷々として徵すべきなり」として後藤祐乘と狩野元信、横谷宗珉と英一蝶、戸張富久と酒井抱一などの関係についてたびたび尋ねている。桑原氏は勝珉と交流があり、技術のことについてたびたび尋ねたというだけあって勝珉のこの抵抗を受け入れなかったのか、同著の『日本装剣金工史』(萩原星文館、昭和十六年)においては彫金家と下絵に関する記述は一切除かれている。

さて、ここで勝珉に関する前述の言葉を踏まえて、勝珉没後に甥の海野美盛(二代)が勝珉の下絵に「天下に名声を馳するに至らしめた二大傑作として挙げた作品のうちの「鬼の宝鈴を曳く図」の胸飾について触れたい。

勝珉の出世作《鬼の宝鈴を曳く図》の胸飾

勝珉の二大傑作といえば、現在知られている作品から見て、誰もが宮内庁三の丸尚蔵館所蔵の《蘭陵王置物》と《太平楽置物》を挙げるであろう。これに反して、勝珉の仕事を最もよく知る一人であろう甥の海野美盛が書画骨董雑誌九十号(大正四年)に寄稿した「故帝室技芸員海野勝珉先生」に、《太平楽置物》にはいっさい触れず、《蘭陵王置物》に先がけて《鬼の宝鈴を曳く図》の胸飾を挙げている。これは美盛によれば、ウィリアム・スタージス・ビゲロウ(註5)が岡倉覚三(天心)、芳崖、橋本雅邦と親交があり、明治二十年頃に西洋婦人の胸飾を制作するための図案を芳崖に依頼し、岡倉に相談してこの図を彫金で制作できる人を捜したところ、ビゲロウとも親交のあった菊屋橋の古道具屋の推薦で海野勝珉に制作を依頼することになった。完成された作品は芳崖の下絵以上の傑作であったのでビゲロウ、フェノロサをはじめ、見た人は皆驚いたという。さらに芳崖の「下繪以上の妙技なるを賞し」たこと、そ(芳崖は明治二十一年没)ので、勝珉は芳崖の親友であった橋本雅邦に一蝶に下書をみせたところ、やはり芳崖の親友であった橋本雅邦に

図6 藤本正義模刻「鬼宝鈴を曳く図首飾」
fig.6 Clasp of ogres pulling a bell, replica by Fujimoto Masayoshi

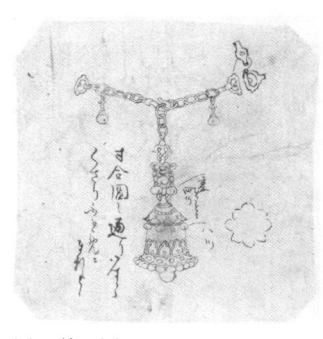

図5 鈴の図
fig.5 Bell

図4 鬼の図
fig.4 Pair of Ogres

してその胸飾はビゲロウが帰国した際に米国に持ち帰り、「ボストン博物館に陳列されている」と記している。そして、勝珉の完成作は芳崖の図案とは同じかたちではなかったと推測できる。この傑作により岡倉らが勝珉の実力を認め、後に東京美術学校の彫金の教員として採用された要因の一つとされている。これらの記述にこの傑作について「幸にも世に出る機會に遭遇した、それはフェノロサ氏清もこれに勝珉の彫金の完成作は未完の仕事となる。それよりは、勝珉が芳崖の図に従って一部を制作してみたものに頼まれて夫人の胸飾り……を彫ったのが、出世作で……芳崖翁は其仕上がりを見ずに死んだが、後に雅邦翁がそれを見て嘆賞した程である。」と記しており、出世作と位置づけている（註6）。ビゲロウが日本で収集した美術品の膨大なコレクションを明治四十四年にボストン美術館に寄贈した中に、現在も伝わる芳崖の下絵が『胸飾図案「鬼寶鈴を牽く」』と題して所蔵品になっている図（図3）が存在する。ここで、明らかにボストン美術館所蔵の芳崖の図案の鈴と鬼が部分的に一致する図案が海野家資料に含まれている（74頁参照、図4、5）ことに注目したい。芳崖の図案には鬼が十四匹混沌とした状況に描かれているが、勝珉のこのうちの二匹だけが再構成されて描かれている。しかも、鈴の寸法、およびその二匹の鬼の寸法が芳崖の図とほぼ一致する。勝珉の死亡を伝える大正四年十月九日の読売新聞の朝刊の記事には「双鬼鐘を引く図」と記され、これにより完成作品の鬼は二匹であったと類推できないだろうか。少なくとも、勝珉の二匹の鬼の図が芳崖の図を参照した図案であることは疑う余地がない。実は、芸大美術館の所蔵品に藤本正義（一八九八—一九七五）による《鬼宝鈴を曳く図首飾》（金工575、縦七・五、横一〇・〇）と題する芳崖の図の右の鬼たちだけを打ち出した模作が収蔵されている（図6）。箱書には「狩野芳崖下図　海野勝珉刻の模」とある。寸法や構図は確かに芳崖の図のとおりに制作されているが、もしこれに左の部分と鈴を加えた首飾りにせよ胸飾りにせよ、当時の装身具としては相応しいとはとても云えない大きさと形状となる。藤本正義は大正十年に東京美術学校金工科を卒業し、模刻は大正十三年に寄贈している。藤本が生まれる前である一八八九年にビゲロウが持ち帰った完成作をもし模刻したとすれば、それは「ボストン博物館で陳列された

作品を借用して模刻したことになるが、それならば「宝鈴」をも作らなければ「鬼宝鈴を曳く図」にはならず、芸大に寄贈した作品は未完の仕事となる。それよりは、勝珉が芳崖の図に従って一部を制作してみたものの、胸飾にした方がふさわしいとして完成させるよりは、もっと整理された図案にした方がふさわしいとして《海野家資料》に残された図案に変更し、芳崖図のとおりの試作の一部が美術学校周辺に残っていたものを藤本が模刻したのではないだろうか。
現物の存在が確認できないが、現存する図案を比べることによって、勝珉が芳崖の図を彫金のアクセサリーに替えたと見なすことができる。「彫金の掟一本でも趣味を尚ぶべきである」とした典型的な例となろう。

続いてこれを機会に《海野家資料》に含まれる下図と東京芸術大学に所蔵される他の資料との関連について紹介したいのが明治三十三年パリ万国博覧会出品下図および大正四年大正天皇即位式と大正五年の裕仁親王立太子礼の際に東京市より東京美術学校に依嘱された衝立の下図である。

明治三十三年パリ万国博覧会出品下図

《海野家資料》に含まれる図案の中で、明治三十三年パリ万国博覧会の巴里博出品組合に提出された図案類がある。「巴里博出品組合蔵記」という割り印が捺され、もう片方の割り印と一致する同じ図案が、組合側の資料とみなすことができる《下図類》と題する資料に含まれている。この《下図類》とは、もともとは明治四十二年四月二十四日に三百円で東京美術学校に買入された九百六十枚の図案であるが、分類や大きさ別に軸装七巻と折本十五冊に表装されたため、軸装の七巻は芸術資料館（大学美術館の前身）の資料となり、十五冊は「和漢書」に組入れ図書館資料となった（註7）。巴里博覧會出品組合とは、明治三十三年パリ万博への出品ためのの事務手続き等を行なう臨時博覧会事務所の承認を得てこれを代行した民間の団体である巴里萬国博覧会出品聯合協会と出品者との仲介を行なった各府県の出品団体の一つである（註8）。

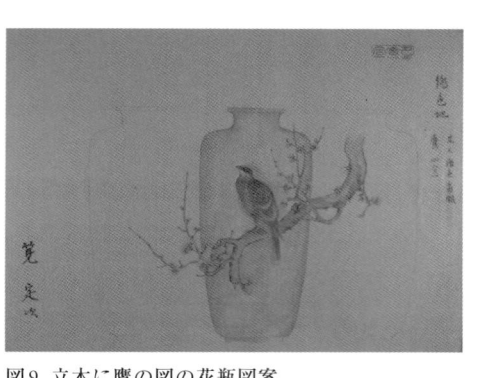

図9 立木に鷹の図の花瓶図案
fig.9 Draft sketch for vase with hawk on a branch

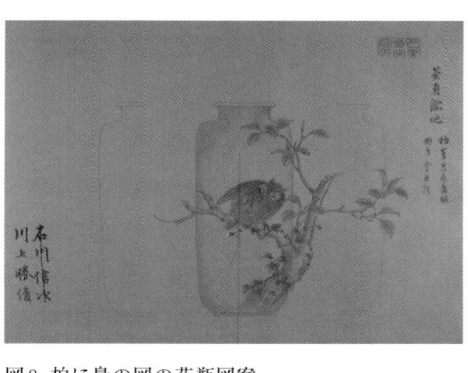

図8 柏に梟の図の花瓶図案
fig.8 Draft sketch for vase with horned owl on oak tree

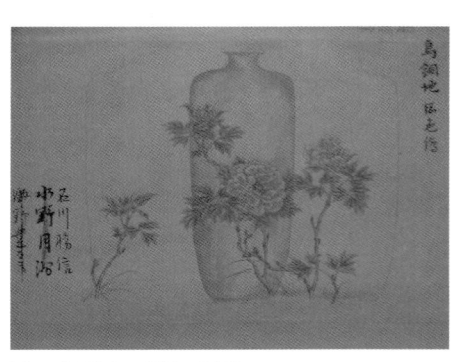

図7 牡丹図の花瓶の図案
fig.7 Draft sketch for vase with peony design

筆者はかつてこれらの図案とパリ万博会場写真や『美術画報 第二臨時増刊 巴里万国博覧会出品製作品』（以下『美術画報』）(註9)の写真と一致する図案を百二十五枚照合し、「明治期の博覧会出品用工芸図案の調査・研究」（『二〇〇一年度鹿島美術研究 年報第十九号別冊』二〇〇二）で報告した。その時の資料の受け入れの経緯についで不明としていたが、香取秀真による西尾卓郎に関する次の記述がこれに当たると思われる。「工商會社の仕事をした白山松哉が東京美術学校の教授になってゐた頃、老人の蔵して居た蒔絵や陶器や木工の下圖類を學校に買上げて貰った事が有った。今學校の文庫に数冊の折本と数巻の巻物に仕立てられてゐるのがそれである。」(『西尾卓郎翁の談話』『金工史談 続篇』日本美術協会報告第二十二輯 昭和六年十一月十三日、『金工史談 続篇』国書刊行会 昭和五十一年)。この談話によれば西尾卓郎は、明治六年のウィーン万国博覧会の時の出品作品の蒐集、荷造りや輸送に携わり、起立工商会社の社員として明治八年のメルボルン博、十一年や二十三年のパリ博などへ出張し、会社解散後は二十五年から林忠正の二十六年シカゴ博で林忠正の随行員となり、その後林の店で作品の整理にあたった。また明治三十三年パリ博の出品組合が二百人の工人に作品を依頼した事があり、その時の製作の世話をした主な人は西尾であったという。白山松哉が東京美術学校の教授を務めたのは、明治三十八年から大正十二年であるため、《下図類》の購入年はこの範囲以内であり、矛盾しない。なお《下図類》という名称で登録されている資料は芸大所蔵品の中でこれが唯一である。

実は上記の談話における下図類が当館の起立工商会社《工芸下図》(一九六九枚 雑美術工芸品525)に該当するかもしれないという指摘が樋田豊次郎著『明治の輸出工芸図案』(京都書院、昭和六十二年)に記されている。これに対しては、《工芸下図》は「折本」や「巻物」に仕立てられておらず、購入された記録がなく、昭和六十年に新規登録された資料であり、香取の記述に合致しない。ただ起立工商会社の下図を西尾卓郎旧蔵の資料として同時期に預かり、形状や大きさがばらばらのペラ状および四冊の簡易綴じの冊子であるために登録が遅れたという可能性はおおいにある。

案は牡丹図案の花瓶(10頁参照)、立木に鷹の図の花瓶の図案および枝の上の木菟の図案(63頁参照)、である。これに該当する「下図類」の牡丹図案の花瓶の図(図7)には「水野月洲」「海野豊太郎」の文字が消されて「石川勝信」と記され、立木に鷹の図案の花瓶〈図8〉は「石川勝信」の文字が消されて「川上勝俊」と記され、立木の木菟の図の花瓶に該当する図〈図9〉は「筧定次工房」と記載されている。枝の上の木菟の図案に該当する「下図類」の図〈図10〉は「勝珉工房」と記載されている。

水野月洲は勝珉の弟子、海野豊太郎は勝珉の長男、石川勝信は滑川貞勝(萩谷勝平門下)の弟子、川上勝俊は萩谷勝平の弟子、筧定次は明治三十五年東京美術学校彫金科卒業生であった。これらの図案のうち、『美術画報』における「石川勝信作牡丹図花瓶」「川上勝俊作木菟花瓶」「田口勝雄作波図花瓶」と題した図(図11)は『美術画報』において「海野勝珉作」の名前が記載されているが「下図類」《海野家資料》には含まれていない図の写真が掲載されており、同博覧会で銀牌を受賞した作品に該当すると思われる。

東京市名所図扇面

当館の《東京市名所図扇面》(東洋画真蹟810)という大正四年十一月十日の御大礼(大正天皇即位式)と五年十一月三日の裕仁親王立太子礼の時に東京市より、東京美術学校に制作を依頼した衝立の下絵がある。彫漆、螺鈿、彫金、陶器、木彫、牙彫、蒔絵などの各種技法により「宮城二重橋」「神田須田町」「日本橋魚市場」「佃島」「芝浦」「上野公園」「浅草観音堂」「向島」「東京砲兵工廠」「東京天文台」「青山練兵場」「四谷見附」「牛込神楽坂」「東京砲兵工廠」「東京帝国大学」「深川木場」の十五区の名所を表したという記録があり、当館にはそのうちの下図十一枚のみが〈東京市名所図扇面〉に収録さている(註10)。収録されているうち海野勝珉が担当した「東京砲兵工廠」の図と見なすことが出来るうちの四図の《海野家資料》に含まれる「巴里博出品組合蔵記」の割り印のある図

図11 海野勝珉作「波図花瓶」図案
fig.11 Draft sketch for vase with wave design, by Unno Shomin

図10 枝の上の木菟の図案
fig.10 Draft sketch for horned owl on a branch

図が《海野家資料》に含まれている（103頁参照）。東京砲兵工廠は現在の東京ドームの場所に位置し、砲兵のみならず明治の鋳金界にとって重要な存在として、東京初の銅像とみなされる靖国神社にある大村益次郎像（大熊氏廣作）をはじめとする銅像や馬上を含む銅像の鋳造が行なわれた場所であった（香取秀真『日本の鋳金』昭和十七年三笠書房）。明治四年竣工、関東大震災で倒壊するまで、東京市内最大の工場として約十万坪の広大な地域にもおよぶ水道橋付近の風景を占領していた名所ではあったが、《海野家資料》にそれを美術の作品のモチーフとした図は珍しい図であるといえよう。ちなみに、年代的に勝珉の最晩年に当たる資料である。

ついでながら《東京市名所図扇面》に含まれている図の中で京橋の「佃島」と題する宮智一男による布目象嵌の下図に「秀静」という署名・捺印がされているが、これは《海野家資料》（9、17頁参照）のほか、当館の《香川勝広資料》（金工1596）の中にもよくみる豊川秀静の署名である。豊川秀静についてわかることが少なく、絵師として活躍した人ではないが、勝珉が顧問をつとめた『日本金工協会役員名簿』（大正元年十二月改選、《香川勝広資料》所収）において、図案部員として記載されているため、金工品の図案に従事した人とみなすことができる。

以上、関連資料との比較の中でいままであまり知られていないいくつかの図案について述べたが、いずれも実作品が確認できない。一般に知られている実作品と照合できる図案は、宮内庁三の丸尚蔵館蔵《浪に鷲図花瓶》（28、29頁参照）や東京国立博物館所蔵《香川勝広資料》に鷲図花瓶》（28、29頁参照）、あるいは当館蔵の《柳馬図巻煙草入》（90、120頁参照）などと数が少なく、本書の公刊によって新たに確認できる作品も期待したい。なお、本書掲載の図と照合されている海野勝珉の作品は、『東京芸術大学芸術資料館 蔵品目録 拓本』（平成五年）に一部掲載されているが、これらの研究は課題として残されている。

最後に、《海野家資料》に含まれている賞状に勝珉の代表作品を除く作品名やその制作を可能にした出品者の情報が記載されているため、ここに一覧表を示し、今後の研究に供したい。

（東京芸術大学大学美術館助教授）

註1 「海野家資料」東京芸術大学大学美術館登録番号 金工1596 主に参照した資料は東京芸術大学大学美術館教官履歴書、「海野教授の卒去」「東京美術学校友会月報」第十四巻第六号 大正四年十一月三十日、「東京名工鑑」（明治十二年、東京府勧業課）、「海野勝珉君還暦祝賀会」、長谷川栄『夏雄と勝珉』（明治十六年、萩原星文館、船越春秀『日本の彫金』三彩社、昭和四十九年、『日本装剣金工史』昭和四十六年、桑原洋次郎『日本装剣金工史』昭和二十三、「勝珉翁近く」読売新聞、大正四年十月九日朝刊、宮内庁三の丸尚蔵館編『明治の彫金——海野勝珉とその周辺』平成十八年九月、ほか。

註2 「東京美術学校一覧 従明治廿九年 至明治三十年」『東京芸術大学百年史 東京美術学校篇 第一巻』昭和六十二年。なお「東京美術学校一覧 従明治廿八年 至明治廿九年」においては、鍛金科の教官は、助教授向井繁太郎、嘱託教員 平田宗之助、全嘱託教員 桜井正次であった。

註3 若山猛『刀装金工事典』雄山閣出版、平成八年、海野美盛「帝室技芸員 海野勝珉先生」『書画骨董雑誌』九十号、大正四年。『明治デザインの誕生——調査研究報告書 温知図録』東京国立博物館 一九九七・三、「勝珉翁近く」読売新聞、大正四年十月九日朝刊、宮内庁三の丸尚蔵館編『明治の彫金——海野勝珉とその周辺』平成十八年九月、ほか。

註4 鍛金技法においては蝋型をつくらず、直接金属をたたいて形を作るため、この文章は「鍛金法に則りて形を作り」とみなすべきであろう。

註5 William Sturgis Bigelow（一八五〇～一九二六）、一八八二年に初来日し、モースやフェノロサと共に日本美術品収集の旅を始める。一八八九年に帰国後、一八九〇年にはボストン美術館理事に就任し、一九一一年には自身のコレクションをボストン美術館に寄贈。

註6 海野清「金工一般と金属彫刻──下」『日本美術』2-2 大正八年七月。

註7 東京芸術大学大学美術館所蔵《下図類》登録記号328-38 751、附属図書館所蔵《下図類》登録記号東洋画模本3745-3

註8 巴里萬国博覧会出品協会残務取扱所刊『千九百年巴里萬国博覧会出品協会報告』一九〇三年。87頁に巴里萬国博覧会出品協会と出品者との仲介を行なった各府県の出品団体名が記載され、「出品組合」と称する団体は「京都府及愛知県聯合七寶出品組合」と「東京出品組合」がある。

註9 『美術画報』第二 臨時増刊 巴里万国博覧会出品製作品』画報社刊、一九〇〇年

註10 『芸大コレクション展 資料はつなぐ——名作と下絵・連作』向井知子・小川真理、細谷誠編、芸大ミュージアムショップ／六文舎 発行二〇〇五年 27ページ参照）。なお、このことについては、小川真理氏より教示いただいた。

海野勝珉賞状一覧（二冊のうち、掲載順序を最後に付した）

年月日	展覧会	出品者区分	作者	作品名	賞	掲載番号
明治二十一年十一月二十五日	東京彫工會第三囘競技會		海野勝珉	彫襯引手二仙人	銀賞票	1-40
明治二十二年五月十三日	日本美術協會美術展覽會	出品人 海野勝珉		銀製鷺烏彫盆	銅牌	1-26
明治二十二年五月五日	日本美術協會美術展覽會	出品人 海野勝珉		銀八角形近江八景彫香箱	銅牌	1-27
明治二十三年十月十七日	東京彫工會第五囘競技會	林九兵衛出品	工人 海野勝珉	素銅彫寒山拾得圖圓額	銀賞票	1-28
明治二十四年十月十一日	東京彫工會第六囘競技會	林九兵衛出品	工人 海野勝珉	鐵彫群狸圖額	朧銀賞票	1-30
明治二十四年五月九日	日本美術協會美術展覽會		海野勝珉	料紙筥嵌入色繪彫舞妓朧銀彫田子浦歌繪卷筥箱彫銅	銅牌	1-29
明治二十五年五月十三日	日本美術協會美術展覽會	林九兵衛出品	製造者 海野勝珉	銀朧銀製秋草流水彫卷筥入（岸光景考案）	二等賞銅牌	1-35
明治二十五年五月十六日	日本美術協會美術展覽會	櫻井いと出品	工人 海野勝珉	金製蟷螂角力艸彫手釦	褒狀一等	1-32
明治二十五年五月十六日	日本美術協會美術展覽會	林九兵衛出品	製造者 海野勝珉	朧銀酸草彫香盒	銅牌	1-31
明治二十五年十一月二十五日	東京彫工會第七囘競技會	林九兵衛出品	製造者 海野勝珉	朧銀鷹架彫唐櫃小筥	銀賞票	1-33
明治二十七年五月七日	日本美術協會春季美術展覽會	櫻井いと出品	製造者 海野勝珉	朧銀鷹架彫筥入（大森獨幹考案）	三等賞銀牌	1-19
明治二十七年五月七日	日本美術協會春季美術展覽會	江澤金五郎出品	製造者 海野勝珉	銀朧彫雀宮故事圖卷筥入（岸光景考案）	三等賞銅牌	1-18
明治二十七年九月十六日	日本美術協會美術展覽會	精工社出品	製造者 海野勝珉	銀彫鷺鴬置物（岸光景考案）	二等賞銀牌	1-34
明治二十七年九月十六日	東京彫工會第九囘競技會	鈴木源助出品	製造者 海野勝珉	朧銀流鮎彫卷筥入	銀賞票	1-36
明治二十八年五月十七日	日本美術協會春季美術展覽會	林九兵衛出品	製造者 海野勝珉	朧銀松猿彫丸額	褒狀一等	1-37
明治二十八年七月十一日	第四囘内國勸業博覽會	林九兵衛出品	製作人 海野勝珉	朧銀鯉魚彫香爐	三等銅賞	2-45
明治二十八年七月十一日	第四囘内國勸業博覽會	杳谷瀧次郎出品	製作人 海野勝珉	朧銀銅彫鷹圖卷煙草入	妙技二等	2-2
明治二十八年七月十一日	第四囘内國勸業博覽會	小池有終出品	製作人 海野勝珉	銀製七賢彫六角香爐	有功二等	1-15
明治二十八年七月十一日	第四囘内國勸業博覽會		海野勝珉	銀製鎚彫鷺置物	審査官 審査官に対する賞	1-39
明治二十九年三月二日		審査官従七位	海野勝珉	銀鎚嵌卷柱圖卷筥入	妙技三等	1-16
明治二十九年五月十三日	日本美術協會美術展覽會	林九兵衛出品	製作人 海野勝珉	朧銀彫琵琶湖圖卷名刺盆	二等賞銀牌	1-14
明治二十九年五月十三日	日本美術協會美術展覽會	林九兵衛出品	製作人 海野勝珉	朧銀彫羅漢圖額		1-38
明治二十九年九月二十日	東京彫工會第十一囘競技會	杳谷滝次郎出品	製造者 海野勝珉	朧銀彫海老沈香壺	銀賞牌	1-13
明治二十九年九月二十日	東京彫工會第十一囘競技會	江澤金五郎出品	製造者 海野勝珉	銀朧銀刻分須磨浦彫卷筥入	銅賞牌	1-21
明治三十年五月十五日	日本美術協會	櫻井いと出品	製造者 海野勝珉	金彫捨扇手釦		
明治三十年五月十五日	日本美術協會	杳谷瀧次郎出品	彫刻者 海野勝珉	金彫鍾馗圖手釦		
明治三十年九月十九日	東京彫工會第十二囘競技會	出品者 海野勝珉	塩津親次作	素銅百鬼夜行圖彫鐔	二等賞牌	1-5
明治三十年九月十九日	東京彫工會第十二囘競技會	杳谷瀧次郎出品	製造者 海野勝珉	金製觀音像置物	協賛褒狀一等	1-8
明治三十年九月十九日	東京彫工會第十二囘競技會		製造者 海野勝珉	朧銀彫秋雨圖卷筥入		

明治三十一年十二月十日	東京彫工會第十三回競技會	櫻井いと出品	製造者 海野勝珉	朧銀彫日本三景圖三種組卷筥入	銀賞牌	1-46
明治三十一年十二月十日	東京彫工會第十三回競技會	櫻井いと出品	製造者 海野勝珉	金製象彫花手釦	銀賞牌	1-9
明治三十一年十二月十日	東京彫工會第十三回競技會	齊藤嘉助出品	製造者 海野勝珉	金製鶴象彫前鉸	褒状一等	1-10
明治三十一年五月十四日	日本美術協會第十三回競技會	櫻井伊登出品	製造者 海野勝珉	銀製宇治景茶壺一対	褒状二等	
明治三十二年五月十三日	日本美術協會春季美術展覽會	齊藤嘉助出品	製造者 海野勝珉	銀製華嚴瀑圖卷筥入	協賛三等賞	1-11
明治三十二年五月十三日	日本美術協會春季美術展覽會	出品者 海野勝珉	川上勝俊作	銀製京都八景圖湯沸急須		
明治三十二年五月十三日	日本美術協會美術展覽會	片岡儀三郎出品	製造者 海野勝珉	黃銅製柏梟彫花瓶	三等賞	1-17
明治三十二年五月十三日	日本美術協會美術展覽會	鈴木源助出品	製造者 海野勝珉	銅製筍彫前鉸		
明治三十二年五月十七日	日本美術協會第十四回競技會	加藤弘之出品	海野勝珉	朧銀製肖像額	一等賞金牌	1-20
明治三十二年九月十三日	東京彫工會第十五回競技會	櫻井伊登出品	製作者 海野勝珉	朧銀狐狸圖手箱	銀賞牌	1-12
明治三十三年五月十五日	日本美術協會春季美術展覽會	片岡儀三郎出品	製作者 海野勝珉、鈴木源助	朧銀製足柄山圖卷筥入	褒状二等	1-3
明治三十三年五月十五日	日本美術協會春季美術展覽會	海野勝珉	加川貫美作	鑄銅觀音像	協賛褒状二等	1-4
明治三十三年五月十五日	日本美術協會春季美術展覽會	岡野信五郎出品	製作者 海野勝珉	朧銀彫寒山拾得卷筥入	三等賞銅牌	1-6
明治三十三年五月十五日	日本美術協會春季美術展覽會	金子直吉出品	製作者 海野勝珉	金製綠毛龜鉸	褒状三等	1-22
明治三十三年五月十五日	日本美術協會春季美術展覽會	櫻井伊登出品	製作者 海野勝珉	朧銀彫三社圖卷筥入	三等賞	1-23
明治三十三年五月十五日	日本美術協會春季美術展覽會	杳谷瀧次郎出品	製作者 海野勝珉	金彫月瀬圖卷筥入	三等賞	1-24
明治三十三年五月十五日	日本美術協會春季美術展覽會	生秀館出品	製作者 海野勝珉	金彫華甲紀念肖像	金賞牌	1-2
明治三十三年五月十五日	日本美術協會春季美術展覽會	島本德兵衞出品	製作者 海野勝珉	金製蝦蟇銕拐圖手釦	銀賞牌	1-25
明治三十三年九月二十三日	東京彫工會第十五回競技會	關口一也出品	製作者 海野勝珉	白金雪景富士手釦	銀賞牌	2-2
明治三十三年九月二十三日	東京彫工會第十五回競技會	金子直吉出品	製作者 海野勝珉	素銅蔦紅葉瓢形花瓶	銅賞牌	2-3
明治三十三年九月二十三日	東京彫工會第十五回競技會	鈴木源助出品	製作者 海野勝珉	朧銀加茂競馬圖香箱	銅賞牌	2-4
明治三十三年九月二十三日	東京彫工會第十五回競技會	齊藤嘉助出品	製作者 海野勝珉	金雨中竹林圖手釦	褒状一等	2-5
明治三十三年九月二十三日	東京彫工會第十五回競技會	柏親舍出品	製作者 海野勝珉	朧銀古今集序文前鉸	銅牌	2-6
明治三十三年九月二十三日	東京彫工會第十五回競技會	島本德兵衞出品	製作者 海野勝珉	朧銀鶴波圖葉筥入	褒状一等	2-7
明治三十三年九月二十三日	東京彫工會第十五回競技會	中村吉兵衞出品	製作者 海野勝珉	朧銀香魚圖前鉸	銅牌	2-6
明治三十三年九月二十三日	東京彫工會第十五回競技會	田口和美出品	製作者 海野勝珉	朧銀三蛙圖前鉸	褒状一等	2-8
明治三十三年九月二十三日	東京彫工會第十五回競技會	杳谷瀧次郎出品	製作者 海野勝珉	烏金墨筆圖前鉸	褒状一等	2-9
明治三十三年九月二十三日	東京彫工會第十五回競技會	金子直吉出品	製作者 海野勝珉	朧銀華嚴瀧圖煙管	褒状一等	2-10
明治三十三年九月二十三日	東京彫工會第十五回競技會	片岡儀三郎出品	製作者 海野勝珉	金梜小鳥圖手釦	褒状一等	2-11
明治三十三年九月二十三日	東京彫工會第十五回競技會	齊藤嘉助出品	製作者 海野勝珉	金大國主圖煙管	金牌	2-12
明治三十四年三月十四日	日本金工協會第壹回競技會	杳谷瀧次郎出品	製作者 海野勝珉	金製鬼鍾馗手釦	銀牌	2-13
明治三十四年三月十四日	日本金工協會第壹回競技會	櫻井伊登出品	製作者 海野勝珉	朧銀製秋雨漁村圖卷葉入	彫金	2-14
明治三十四年三月十四日	日本金工協會第壹回競技會	金子直吉出品	製作者 海野勝珉	金製竹林手釦	彫金	
明治三十四年三月十四日	日本金工協會第壹回競技會	櫻井伊登出品	製作者 海野勝珉	朧銀製古今集序文意前鉸	彫金 銅牌	

年月日	展覧会名	出品者	製作者	作品名	賞	番号
明治三十四年三月十四日	日本金工協會第壹回競技會	島本徳兵衛出品	製作者 海野勝珉	彫金朧銀製鯉圖前鋲	銅牌	2-15
明治三十四年六月二十二日	日本美術協會美術展覽會	齊藤嘉助出品	製作者 海野勝珉	彫金烏銅四所金観櫻圖煙管	一等賞褒状	2-16
明治三十四年九月二十日	農商務省聯合共進會（新潟）	豊田光古出品	製作者 海野勝珉	彫金朧銀製波二鶴圖葉入	褒状一等賞	2-18
明治三十四年十一月一日	関西美術會：京都彫技會聯合秋季展覽會	杢谷瀧次郎出品	製作者 海野勝珉	彫金金鋼鉄張一笑圖煙管	二等賞銀牌	2-19
明治三十五年九月十四日	東京彫工會第十七回競技會	鈴木源助出品	製作者 海野勝珉	白金製櫻花形手釦	一等賞	2-20
明治三十五年九月十四日	東京彫工會第十七回競技會	齊藤嘉助出品	製作者 海野勝珉	花瓶　銀製	感謝状	
明治三十五年十一月十四日	日本美術協會美術展覽會	杢谷瀧次郎出品	製作者 海野勝珉	朧銀製瀧虎圖手函	銀賞牌	2-21
明治三十五年十一月二十二日	日本彫工會第十八回競技會	出品者	製作者 海野勝珉	朧銀銀製孔雀圖名刺盆	銅賞牌	2-26
明治三十五年十一月二十二日	日本美術協會美術展覽會	櫻井榮藏出品	製作者 海野勝珉、鈴木源助	銀朧銀彫住吉圖卷葉函	二等賞銀牌	2-22
明治三十六年十二月六日	東京彫工會第十八回競技會	杢谷滝次郎出品	製作者 海野勝珉、前澤定次郎	三社意匠入朧銀彫鹿前鋲　金製鳩彫緒締	協賛賞状	2-23
明治三十六年七月一日	第五回内國勧業博覽會	杢谷滝次郎出品	製作者 海野勝珉、池田光玉	朧銀製清流香魚彫卷葉入	三等賞銅牌	2-27
明治三十六年七月一日	第五回内國勧業博覽會		海野勝珉	銅製メダル　帝國大學総長山川博士肖像	一等賞金牌	2-24
明治三十七年五月十七日	第五回内國勧業博覽會		海野勝珉	彫金田口大學教授肖像メダル	協賛賞状	2-28
明治三十七年七月十八日	第五回内國勧業博覽會		海野勝珉	金製山水時計	褒状一等	2-29
明治三十七年九月十八日	東京彫工會第十八回競技會	江澤金五郎出品	製作者 海野勝珉	朧銀製卷葉入	褒状一等	2-31
明治三十七年九月十八日	日本彫工會第貳回競技會	杢谷瀧次郎出品	製作者 海野勝珉	銀製七福神彫扇面額	銀賞牌	2-37
明治三十七年九月十八日	日本彫工會第貳回競技會	廣部清兵衞出品	製作者 海野勝珉	金製田子ノ浦圖手釦	金牌	2-32
明治三十七年九月十八日	日本彫工會第貳回競技會	杢谷瀧次郎出品	製作者 海野勝珉	銀製和歌浦卷葉入	金牌	2-38
明治三十七年九月十八日	日本金工協會第貳回競技會	藤本萬作出品	製作者 海野勝珉	日廻草銀製香爐	銀牌	2-33
明治三十七年九月十八日	日本金工協會第貳回競技會	大西榮輔出品	製作者 海野勝珉	朧銀神圖彫刻額	銀牌	2-40
明治三十七年九月二十八日	日本金工協會第貳回競技會	金子直吉出品	製作者 海野勝珉	矢ノ根五郎圖赤銅前鋲	銀牌	2-41
明治三十八年七月二十八日	日本金工協會第三回競技會	片岡儀三郎出品	製作者 海野勝珉	花鳥圖銀製花瓶	銀牌	2-42
明治三十八年七月二十八日	日本金工協會第三回競技會	闘口一也出品	製作者 海野勝珉、海野珉乘	山水圖金製手釦	銅牌	2-43
明治三十八年七月二十八日	日本金工協會第三回競技會	金工協和會出品	製作者 海野勝珉	扇面地板合作五節句横額	銅牌	2-44
明治三十八年九月十八日	日本金工協會第三回競技會	片岡儀三郎出品	製作者 海野勝珉	金白金彫桜花勝蟲圖手釦	銀賞牌	2-45
明治三十八年九月十八日	東京彫工會第二十回競技會	江澤金五郎出品	製作者 海野勝珉	朧金彫刻秋月山水圖卷葉入		2-41
明治三十八年九月十三日	東京彫工會第二十回競技會	杢谷瀧次郎出品	製作者 海野勝珉	朧銀彫松島圖彫刻卷葉入	銀賞牌	
明治三十八年九月二十日	東京彫工會第二十回競技會	関口一也出品	製作者 海野勝珉	烏金鯉魚彫刻前鋲	銅賞牌	1-42
明治三十九年五月十八日	日本美術協會第三十九回美術展覽會特別會員	江澤金五郎出品	製作者 海野勝珉	金製月宮殿彫刻手釦	功労金賞牌	1-1

年月日	展覧会	出品者	製作者	作品	賞	番号
明治三十九年五月十八日	日本美術協會第三十九回美術展覽會	金子直吉出品	製作者 海野勝珉	宣德彫福壽意煙管	技藝褒状三等	1-43
明治三十九年五月十八日	日本美術協會第三十九回美術展覽會	齊藤嘉助出品	製作者 海野勝珉	白金製日本三景彫時計	技藝銅賞牌	1-44
明治三十九年五月十八日	日本美術協會第三十九回美術展覽會	金子直吉出品	製作者 海野勝珉	金彫雁前鋜		
明治三十九年七月二十八日	東京彫工會第二十一回競技會	江澤金五郎出品	製作者 海野勝珉	朧銀鶯柳象嵌巻葉入	銅牌	1-47
明治三十九年七月二十八日	東京彫工會第二十一回競技會	桜井栄蔵出品	製作者 海野勝珉	金白金朝顔末廣彫煙鍵釦		1-48
明治三十九年九月十六日	東京彫工會第二十一回競技會	斉藤嘉助出品	製作者 海野勝珉	金白金若松彫煙管		
明治三十九年九月十六日	東京彫工會第二十一回競技會	斉藤嘉助出品	製作者 海野勝珉	金白金蘭彫煙管		
明治三十九年九月十六日	東京彫工會第二十一回競技會	片岡儀三郎出品	製作者 海野勝珉	金烏金彫山櫻煙管	銀賞牌	1-50
明治三十九年九月十六日	東京彫工會第二十一回競技會	片岡儀三郎出品	製作者 海野勝珉	金製野馬圖手釦	金賞牌	1-51
明治三十九年九月十六日	東京彫工會第二十一回競技會	片岡儀三郎出品	製作者 海野勝珉	朧銀彫雀蛤卷葉入	褒状一等	
明治三十九年十二月四日	凱旋紀念五二共進會	出品人 江澤金五郎	協賛人 海野勝珉	鐵製臺前鋜	出陳に対する感謝状	1-52
明治四十年七月六日	東京勸業博覽會	出品人 海野勝珉	自作	銀製瀑布圖卷葉入	褒状褒状	1-53
明治四十年九月二十一日	東京彫工會第二十二回競技會	櫻井栄蔵出品	製作者 海野勝珉	朧銀彫朝夕之意巻葉箱	協賛賞状	1-54
明治四十一年六月十三日	日本金工協會第四十二回美術展覽會	杳谷瀧次郎出品	製作者 海野勝珉	銀製蔦羅小禽彫刻大花盤	協賛銅賞牌	1-55
明治四十一年六月十三日	日本美術協會第四十二回美術展覽會	江澤金五郎出品	製作者 海野勝珉	朧銀彫刻牧童圖巻莨函	銀賞牌	1-56
明治四十一年六月十三日	日本美術協會第四十二回美術展覽會	櫻井栄蔵出品	製作者 海野勝珉	朧朧銀彫刻嵌巻煙草函　楼閣山水		1-57
明治四十一年六月二十日	日本金工協會第五回競技會	金子直吉出品	製作者 海野勝珉	金彫蘭陵王圖手釦　錦鶏圖	金賞牌	
明治四十一年六月十三日	日本彫工會第二十三回競技會	杳谷瀧次郎出品	製作者 海野勝珉	銀彫卷煙艸入　唐嵜圖	銀賞牌	1-58
明治四十一年六月十五日	東京彫工會第二十三回競技會	海野兼次郎出品	製作者 海野勝珉	銀彫卷煙艸入　月下洗馬圖	銅賞牌	1-59
明治四十一年六月十五日	東京彫工會第二十三回競技會	海野兼次郎出品	自作	銀彫花瓶　蘆鷺圖	褒状一等	
明治四十二年六月十五日	東京彫工會第二十四回競技會	島本徳兵衛出品	製作者 海野勝珉	朧銀彫花瓶　枯木寒鴉圖	記念状	1-60
明治四十二年六月十五日	東京彫工會第二十四回競技會		製作者 海野勝珉	孔雀尾彫刻金指環　石上秋聲圖	記念状	
明治四十二年七月二十八日	東京彫工會第二十四回競技會	金子直吉出品	製作者 海野勝珉	鮎彫刻朧銀前鋜	銀牌	1-63
明治四十二年九月十三日	日本金工協會第六回競技會	江澤金五郎出品	製作者 海野勝珉	朧銀彫晩秋山家圖巻煙草入	金牌	1-64
明治四十二年九月十三日	東京美術工藝展覽會	江澤金五郎出品	製作者 海野勝珉	浪二鷲ノ圖彫刻銀花瓶	銀賞牌	1-65
明治四十二年十二月三日	日本美術協會第四十四回美術展覽會	鈴木茂八出品	製作者 海野勝珉	朧銀地板孔雀彫箱	銀賞牌	1-66
明治四十三年五月六日	東京美術及美術工藝展覽會	宮本勝出品	製作者 海野勝珉	銀彫小禽牡丹菊圖花瓶		1-71
明治四十三年五月六日	東京美術及美術工藝展覽會	櫻井栄蔵出品		朧銀巻煙草入彫刻　寒江獨釣圖	技藝一等賞	1-72

管理番号情報

下記は掲載図の東京芸術大学大学美術館における管理番号情報である。下絵および拓本はすべて登録番号「金工1597」に含まれ、「写生下絵」画帖（a）あるいは「巻子下図」（s）ごとの番号およびその中の順番を示す番号を記した。なお、拓本については番号が付されていない。

The following numbers are to specify the inventory sub-numbers [album (a) or scroll(s) number - numerical order within the album or scroll] of the sketches illustrated, among The University Art Museum inventory number 'Metal Works no. 1597'

ページ番号／枝番号（複数の場合は・頁内上・右から順に下左へ）
page/sub-number. (from upper right to lower left)

花瓶図案
Flower Vase Designs

8／s1-24, 9／s1-5, 10／a1-26, 11／s1-20, 12／s3-16・3-17, 13／s2-26・s2-27, 14／s4-3・s2-19, 15／s4-4・s2-18, 16／s1-11・s2-3, 17／s1-3・s1-19, 18／a1-29・1-30, 19／s3-18・a1-15, 20／s2-7・a1-17, 21／s2-8・a1-18, 22／s3-1・s3-2, 23／s1-26, 24／s2-24・a1-13・s2-25, 25／s2-22・s2-23, 26／s3-7, 27／s3-8, 28-29／a15裏-21・a15裏-20, 30-33／s3-3, 34-35／s3-4, 36-37／s3-9, 38／s3-11

種々図案
Various Designs

39／a2-13, 40／a2-27・a2-43・a15-8, 41／a2-43・a15-17・a15-17・a8-2, 42-45／a2-13, 46／a15-10・a15-10・a2-49, 47／a15-10・a2-25, 48／a5-18, 49／a5-18, 50／a18-9・a18-8・a5-17, 51／a2-6・a5-17, 52／a2-5・s1-16・a2-41・a2-41, 53／a2-29, 54／a2-2, 55／a2-2, 56／a19-12, 57／a19-12・a8-8・a19-13・a19-13, 58／a2-31・a2-32, 59／a2-31・a2-32, 60／a3-12・a2-18・a6-8・a6-8・a6-8・a6-8, 61／a2-18, 62／a2-40・a2-35・a2-38・a2-38, 63／a2-3・a2-3・a2-3・a1-31, 64／a19-13・a2-37, 65／a2-39・a2-37, 66-69／s福地復一考案「網引図」, 70／a21-6, 71／a16-23・a13-20, 72／a21-8・a9-5・a9-5・a8-16, 73／a21-8・a18-5・a9-5・a9-5, 74／a9-18・a11-4・a6-13・a11-4・a9-5・a9-18, 75／a21-8・a11-4・a21-6・a11-2, 76／a21-4・a8-5・a8-12・a14裏-68, 77／a1-36・a8-2・a1-36, 78-79／a1-3, 80／a1-10・a21-12・a8-13・a8-12・a8-13・a1-10, 81／a21-12・a18-25, 82-83／s反魂香, 84-85／s3-14, 86-87／s3-15, 88／a20-10・a16-25, 89／a16-25・s1-29, 90／a6-2・a8-5・a8-5, 91／a14-28・a14-2・a18-5・a14-3・a14-28・a14-25・a8-5, 92／a6-4・a15-8・a20-15, 93／a4-11・a6-2・a20-10, 94／a1-2, 95／a1-2, 96／a12-19・a1-2・a1-5・a12-19, 97／a6-16・a15-2・a18-19・a5-2・a16-32, 98／s12-2・s12-1・s12-2, 99／s12-2・s12-3・s12-4, 100／s5-3・s1-31, 101／a9-3・s1-32, 102／a21-18・a1-8・a12-19, 103／a21-18, 104／a21-18

謝辞
Acknowledgments

本書刊行にあたりご協力をいただきました、
ボストン美術館のジョー・アール氏に深く感謝申し上げます。

Special thanks to Mr. Joe Earle of the Museum of Fine Arts, Boston
for his cooperation towards this study.

海野勝珉（うんのしょうみん）
下絵・資料集
東京芸術大学大学美術館所蔵

発行日　　2007年8月6日　　初版第1刷発行

編著者　　横溝廣子
発行者　　今東成人
発行所　　東方出版株式会社
　　　　　〒543-0052　大阪市天王寺区大道1-8-15
　　　　　TEL.06-6779-9571　FAX.06-6779-9573

撮　影　　寺島郁雄
　　　　　柴田明蘭
編　集　　福田綾美（ライムワークス）
デザイン　坂本佳子（大向デザイン事務所）
印　刷　　泰和印刷株式会社

2007 Printed in Japan
乱丁・落丁本はお取り換えします。
ISBN 978-4-86249-061-2 C0071

SKETCHES OF UNNO SHOMIN
— WITHIN THE COLLECTION OF THE UNIVERSITY ART MUSEUM,
TOKYO NATIONAL UNIVERSITY OF FINE ARTS AND MUSIC

Edited in August, 2007

Author: YOKOMIZO Hiroko
Publisher: IMAHIGASHI Shigeto
Publishing Office:　TOHO SHUPPAN Publishing Co., Ltd.
　　　　　　　　　　Daido 1-8-15, Tennoji-ku, Osaka, 543-0052 Japan
　　　　　　　　　　Tel 06-6779-9571　Fax 06-6779-9573
Photographers:　　 TERASHIMA Ikuo
　　　　　　　　　　SHIBATA Akira
Editor: FUKUDA Ayami (LIME WORKS)
Book Designer: SAKAMOTO Yoshiko(OHMUKAI DESIGN OFFICE)
Printer: TAIWA PRINT Co., Ltd.

Draft Sketches with Sights of Tokyo for Fan Paintings

The 'Draft Sketches with Sights of Tokyo for Fan Paintings' (Eastern Paintings no.810) among our Museum's collection were created for the screen commissioned by the Tokyo City to Tokyo Fine Arts School, to commemorate the Enthronement Ceremony of Emperor Taisho on November 10th, 1915, and the Investiture as Crown Prince (*Rittaishi no Rei*) of Prince Hirohito (later Emperor Showa) on November 3rd, 1916. It was a screen with various techniques such as *choshitsu* (carved lacquer), *raden* (mother of pearl inlay), ceramic, wood carving, ivory carving, *makie*, metal carving, etc. used to depict 15 famous sights of Tokyo. The sights were Nijubashi by the Imperial Castle, Kanda Suda-cho, Nihonbashi fish market, Tsukudajima, Shibaura, Tokyo astronomical observatory, Aoyama parade ground, Yotsuya-mitsuke, Ushigome Kagurazaka, Tokyo artillery factory, Tokyo Imperial University, Ueno Park, Asakusa Konnondo, Mukojima, and Fukagawa Kiba, but only 11 of the sketches exist within the 'Draft Sketches with Sights of Tokyo for Fan Paintings'. However, one of the sketches that was not included was the sketch for Unno Shomin's work, the Tokyo artillery factory, is included within the 'Unno Family Material' (p.103). The Tokyo artillery factory was located where the Tokyo Dome (Korakuen) stands now, and not only did it manufacture artillery, but it was a very important place for metal casting of the Meiji era. The first bronze statue in Tokyo, the OMURA Masujiro statue by OKUMA Ujihiro, which stands in the Yasukuni Shrine grounds, and many other statues were cast within this factory. It was constructed in 1871, and until it was destroyed in the great earthquake of 1923, it was the largest factory in the Tokyo city occupying 330,000 square meters. At the time it was a famous sight of the Suidobashi area, and the work by the sketch within the 'Unno Family Material' would not only be a rare work of art depicting this, but also one of Shomin's latest works.

The sketches introduced in this essay are meaningful in their relationship to other materials, but completed metal works are yet to be confirmed. Among the designs that can be matched with existing works are the 'Pair of vases with design of falcon and waves', (pp.28, 29) in The Museum of the Imperial Collections, Sannomaru Shozokan, and the 'Metal panel, Bugaku Dance Genjoraku' (p.72) in the Tokyo National Museum, or the 'Cigar case with design of willow and horses' (pp.90, 120) in The University Art Museum, Tokyo National University of Fine Arts and Music. We are hoping that this publication will lead us to more actual works. As of rubbings that were taken from actual objects, other than those in this book, a number of them are illustrated in the *Tokyo Geijutsu Daigaku Geijutsu Shiryokan Zohin Mokuroku-Takuhon* (1993), and research on these are yet to be done. Last of all, we add a list of the certificates of merit included in the 'Unno Family Material' (in Japanese, p. 146–149) showing the exhibitor's names who supported Shomin's work for the benefit of future research.

(Associate Professor, Tokyo National University of Fine Arts and Music)

in the 'Unno Family Materials', more appropriate for a breast ornament. Therefore, Shomin's incomplete half was probably left somewhere around the school, where FUJIMOTO Masayoshi could easily get access to.

If so, this can be considered as a typical and the most important example where Shomin emphasized taste as a rule in metal work.

I would like to take this opportunity to introduce some of the designs in the 'Unno Family Materials' in relation to other materials in the Tokyo National University of Fine Arts. Namely, design sketches for objects to be exhibited in the 1900 Paris International Exposition, and a design sketch for the screen commissioned by the Tokyo City to Tokyo Fine Arts School, to commemorate the Enthronement Ceremony of Emperor Taisho in 1915, and the Investiture as Crown Prince (*Rittaishi no Rei*) of Prince Hirohito (later Emperor Showa) in 1916.

Design sketches for 1900 Paris International Exposition

Among the 'Unno Family Materials', there are a few designs that have half of a seal impression of The Paris World Exposition Exhibiter's Union. The same design with the other half of the seal impression is within the designs that the same Union compiled, titled 'Shitazurui' (various designs) within both the University Art Museum and the Library of the Tokyo National University of Fine Arts. The 'Shitazurui' are 960 designs mounted on 7 scrolls and 15 albums that were purchased by the Tokyo Fine Arts School in 1909.

According to KATORI Hotsuma, the following accounts on NISHIO Takuro are probably about the 'Shitazurui'; "When SHIRAYAMA Shosai who used to work for Kosho Kaisha, was professor of the Tokyo Fine Arts School, the design sketches of *makie*, ceramic and woodwork that Nishio owned were purchased by the School. The albums and scrolls in the School library are this material. (*Nishio Takuro no Danwa, Nihon Bijutsu Kyokai Hokoku* no.22, 1931.) According to this article, NISHIO Takuro worked in the collection, packing and transportation of the exhibits for the Vienna International Exposition of 1873, and acted as an employee of the Kiriu Kosho Gaisha (First Manufacturing Company) in the 1875 Melbourne Exposition, the 1878 and 1890 Paris International Expositions, and after the Company dissolves, since 1892 he worked with HAYASHI Tadamasa, and attended Hayashi at the World's Columbian Exposition in Chicago, and after that, he worked to dispose of Hayashi's shop's stock. On the occasion of the 1900 Paris International Exposition, the Exhibiter's Union commissioned 200 craftsmen to create works for the Exposition, and the person that assisted this was NISHIO Takuro. SHIRAYAMA Shosai was professor at the Tokyo Fine Arts School from 1905 to 1023, and the purchase of these 'Shitazurui' is within this period.

The designs with seal impression of The Paris World Exposition Exhibiter's Union within the 'Unno Family Material' are the draft sketch for vase with peony design (p.10), the draft sketch for vase with horned owl on oak tree and the draft sketch for vase with hawk on a branch (p.18), and the draft sketch for horned owl on a branch (p.63). The sketches that match these within the 'Shitazurui' are fig.7 to 10, with names of the person who was to create the exhibited work. Fig.7 has the names MIZUNO Gesshu (Shomin's pupil) and UNNO Toyotaro (Shomin's eldest son) erased and changed to ISHIKAWA Katsunobu (HAGIYA Katsuhira's pupil NAMEKAWA Sadakatsu's pupil). Fig.8 has the name KAWAKAMI Katsutoshi (HAGIYA Katsuhira's pupil), Fig.9 has the name KAKEI Sadaji (student of the Tokyo Fine Arts School metal carving section), and fig.10 has the words "Shomin-kobo" (Shomin's workshop).

The only design in the 'Shitazurui' with the name UNNO Shomin is fig.11, which is probably for the vase in the photograph of the 'Silver Vase with Picture of Waves' in the *Extra Issue No. 2. of Fine Arts Magazine containing Illustrations and Descriptions of Products of The Paris World Exposition Exhibiter's Union,* which is the same title as his work that received a silver medal at the exposition.

chisel work when creating the design. (*Shoga Kotto Zasshi* 32, 1911). "Kuwabara's book" is probably the *Soken Kinko-dan* (1904) by KUWABARA Yojiro. The chapter titled "Chokin-ko to shitae-shi" (Metal carving craftsmen and designers) within the *Soken Kinko-dan* states that master metal craftsmen often engaged with master painters of the same era, and received help in their designs, such as GOTO Yujo, and KANO Motonobu, YOKOYA Somin and HANABUSA Iccho, TOBARI Tomihisa and SAKAI Hoitsu. KUWABARA Yoichiro was acquainted with Shomin, and often asked him about metal techniques, and probably because of this, he did not mention anything about designs in his next book *Nihon Soken Kinkoshi* (1941).

Based on these words of Shomin, I want to introduce the words of Shomin's nephew UNNO Yoshimori II stating that two masterpieces brought fame to Shomin. The first was the breast ornament depicting ogres pulling a precious bell, and the second was the mentioned Raryo-o figure.

Shomin's work which won his distinction

Presently, Shomin's two major works would be considered by many as the Raryo-o and the Taiheiraku figures in the Museum of Imperial Collections, Sannomaru Shozokan. In contrast, Shomin's nephew UNNO Yoshimori II, who must have been one of the closest persons knowing Shomin's work, wrote about Shomin in *Shoga Kotto-Zasshi* vol.90 (1915), and did not mention the Taiheraku figure at all. Yoshimori claimed that the first work that gained Shomin's fame was the breast ornament depicting ogres pulling a precious bell, that was designed by KANO Hogai. William Sturgis BIGELOW consulted OKAKURA Tenshin about who might be appropriate to create a metal piece based on this design, around 1887. The completed work by Shomin is said to be a masterpiece surpassing the original design, and Bigelow, Fenollosa, etc., and the others that observed it, were all astonished by its completion. Because Hogai died before the completed piece was finished, Shomin showed the finished piece to Hogai's close friend HASHIMOTO Gaho, who appraised the work as technically excellent beyond Hogai's design. According to Yoshimori, the breast ornament was brought to America by Bigelow, and was exhibited in the Boston Museum. These accounts suggest that the completed work by Shomin was not exactly the same as the design by Hogai. Furthermore, by this masterpiece, OKAKURA Tenshin recognized Shomin's ability, leading to his employment to the Tokyo Fine Arts School. Shomin's son UNNO Kiyoshi also referred to this work as the piece which won Shomin's distinction, but not as a request by Bigelow, but by Fenollosa.

The vast collection of works Bigelow brought from Japan was donated to the Museum of Fine Arts, Boston in 1911. Among this, the 'Design for a Clasp' by KANO Hogai (fig.3) exists, but the whereabouts of the completed metal work by Shomin is yet to be confirmed. At this point, I would like to compare Hogai's design to one of the designs in the 'Unno Family Materials' (p. 74, fig.4, 5). In Hogai's design, there are 14 ogres in a chaotic state, whereas Shomin's design selects two of them, almost exactly the same size as the ones selected from Hogai's design. The bell is also the same size as in Hogai's design. As the obituary in the Yomiuri Shimbun newspaper of October 9th, 1915, refers to the work to be "a pair of ogres pulling a bell", Shomin's completed work was probably done according to the design left in the 'Unno Family Materials'.

However, there is a work within the University Art Museum collection titled "Neck ornament of ogres pulling a bell" (7.5 × 10.0 cm.), created according to the right half of KANO Hogai's design in size and shape, without any bell (fig.6). It is a reproduction of the same work by Shomin, created by FUJIMOTO Masayoshi (1898–1975). However, if this was completed according to Hogai's design, with the other half and the bell, it would probably be too large and inappropriate as either a neck or breast ornament for the time. FUJIMOTO Masayoshi graduated from The Tokyo Fine Arts School metal technique section in 1921, and donated this reproduction to the school in 1924.

Bigelow returned to the U.S. in 1889, which was before FUJIMOTO Masayoshi was born, and therefore if he had the chance to see Shomin's completed work, he would have had to go to the trouble in borrowing the work that was "exhibited in the Boston Museum", and if this was the case, his reproduction work donated to the Tokyo Fine Arts School would be incomplete. It would be easier to consider that Shomin created the right half according to Hogai's design, but decided to rearrange the design to the one

Sketch album 5	27.2 × 19.4	(cigarette cases, dishes, etc)
Sketch album 6	27.2 × 19.3	(cigarette cases, dishes, etc , birds, animals, etc.)
Sketch album 7	27.2 × 19.4	(plants)
Sketch album 8	27.2 × 19.3	
Sketch album 9	27.2 × 19.3	
Sketch album10	27.2 × 19.3	
Sketch album11	27.1 × 19.2	(sword guards, rubbings)
Sketch album12	27.1 × 19.2	
Sketch album13	17.0 × 24.4	(sword fittings of various craftsmen)
Sketch album14	17.0 × 24.4	(sword fittings of various craftsmen)
Sketch album15	22.5 × 15.8	Sketches from 1906–March 1907, (vases)
Sketch album16	15.0 × 22.0	
Sketch album17	15.0 × 22.0	
Sketch album18	15.0 × 22.0	
Sketch album19	32.0 × 23.5	(plants and birds)
Sketch album20	32.0 × 23.5	(animals, birds, fish and insects)
Sketch album21	32.0 × 23.5	(deities and Buddhas, legendary wizards, and human figures)
Sketch scroll 1	37.5 × 1793.7	Vase Designs with flower and landscapes, (27 designs)
Sketch scroll 2	37.5 × 1576.0	Vase Designs for the Imperial Household Ministry, (34 designs)
Sketch scroll 3	44.0 × 909.8	Silver Vase Designs, (18 designs)
Sketch scroll 4	47.6 × 940.6	Silver vase designs, (12 designs) for Kangyo Bank
Sketch scroll 5	50.2 × 714.6	Vases with landscape designs, 9 designs
Sketch scroll 6	50.7 × 274.0	Ivy sketches
Sketch scroll	sketch 77.3 × 75.0	(scene from the fable "Hangonko", Han Dynasty Emperor Wudi and his wife Lee appearing among incense smoke after she has past away) (p. 83)
Sketch scroll	sketch 53.5 × 65.7	Net fishing design by FUKUCHI Mataichi (p.66, 67)

Among the sketches, there are many signed as Okyo (MARUYAMA Okyo), Keibun (MATSUMURA Keibun), Tanyu-sai (KANO Tanyu), Iccho (HANABUSA Iccho), and others painters, including printed material. Among the rubbings there are works inscripted as "Miyamoto Niten-i Shomin-sen" (Shomin carves according to MIYAMOTO Niten's design), "Okyo-no-zu-ni-narau Teishitsu-gigeiin Hoshu-so Shomin-koku" (Imperial Court Artist Hoshu-so Shomin carves according to MARUYAMA Okyo's painting), "Mokkeiga-Shomin-koku" (Shomin carves MOKKEI's painting), "Beisen-ga-Shomin-koku" (Shomin carves KUBOTA Beisen's painting), "Katei-ga-Shomin-koku" (Shomin carves TAKI Katei's painting), "Gyokusho-ga-Shomin-koku" (Shomin carves KAWABATA Gyokusho's painting), or "Shomin-to-Kason-zu" (Shomin's chisel, SUZUKI Kason's painting), and among the metal plates in the Tokyo Fine Arts School (pp.105–119) their are inscriptions reading "Okyo-i-Shomin-koku" (Shomin carves MARUYAMA Okyo's design), "Riryumin-i-Shomin-koku" (Shomin carves Riryumin's design), showing that Shomin often expressed various painters' styles in his metal carving techniques. According to Shomin's sense, this was done with pride, showing his skillful techniques in various famous painters' styles. Shomin's following words about sketches shows his attitude;

"After the Haitō edict restricting the wearing of a sword, metal carving creating sword furnishings declined and these techniques had to be used to create other objects. Discernment of clients also declined, and there were people that even brought draft sketches requesting to have it created in metalwork. As I have said, paintings have painting's rules, and metalwork has metalwork's rules, and the taste should be respected in each rule, but at that time this was unthinkable, and metalwork fell into a pitiful situation competing in gaudiness....", "Kuwabara's book states that Somin (YOKOYA Somin) created work with Iccho's (HANABUSA Iccho) designs, and Ichijo's (GOTO Ichijo) work was by Yosai's (KIKUCHI Yosai) design, but these are the words of someone who does not know practical work. One needing to have a design drawn for them by someone else, can not be considered as a master. Work created with a metal chisel will not be something interesting, if one does not know the characteristics of

Tokyo Fine Arts School the next year, and in 1896, he is appointed as an Imperial Court Artist (Member of the Consultative Board of Fine Arts of the Imperial Court), and acts as professor of both the metal carving and metal hammering sections at the Tokyo Fine Arts School, until the sections were merged.

In the Paris International Exposition of 1900, he received silver medal for a silver vase with wave design, and also exhibited another figure depicting a court dancer, Taiheiraku. He receives a gold medal at the Nihon Bijutsu Kyokai exhibition in 1905 for a silver vase with flowers and bird design (sketch on p.16). In the Japan British Exhibition of 1910, he received an honorary prize for a silver vase with ivy and small bird design. He died on October 8th, 1915 at the age of 72.

Few documents on Shomin mention that he studied under and was greatly influenced by a master of wrought iron named MYOCHIN Ki-no Yoshiomi, who created armor for the Mito domain. (FUNAKOSHI Shunmin, *Nihon no Chokin*, 1974). The *Tokyo Bijutsu Gakko Ichiran* which is an annual handbook of the Tokyo Fine Arts School lists UNNO Shomin as the professor of both the metal carving section and the metal hammering section since the year after the metal hammering section was established in 1895, until both of these sections were merged together in 1905. The reason why I am emphasizing these facts is because there was a distinct discrimination between the metal carving craftsmen and the metal hammering craftsmen at the time. The metal hammering craftsmen ordinarily created the base for the metal carving craftsmen's work, which was embossed or inlayed by the metal carving craftsmen, and there are many existing pieces created in this way. However, the reputation Shomin received about his Raryoo figure in the newspapers, was that the metal hammering technique used in this work was a skill that other ordinary metal carving craftsmen did not have, and to create this kind of figure without the help of a metal casting craftsmen was unheard of before, astonishing the learned people. The metal carving craftsmen traditionally used only the metal chisels, and did not use the techniques of the casting or hammering craftsmen. If they used both, they were considered as disorderly and dishonorable craftsmen, and if they used hammering techniques exceeding high relief embossing for the majority of the work, they were looked down on as metal hammering craftsmen. Shomin's Raryo-o was highly praised as the first metal carving work using metal hammering techniques as its major feature, and opened the eyes of the metal carving craftsmen that were only creating small objects.

In other words, the Raryo-o figure was an epoch making attempt, that might have been considered dishonorable because of the usage of both metal carving and hammering techniques. The results were eye-opening for the metal craftsmen of the era, and the Tokyo Fine Arts School highly praised this attempt, printing a large photograph of this Raryo-o figure and UNNO Shomin himself in his obituary in the School's monthly bulletin (fig.2).

The 'Unno Family Materials'

As we have looked upon the achievements of UNNO Shomin, next we will introduce some materials that were left in his family, focusing on several design sketches among them.

The 'Unno Family Materials' includes 8 scrolls, 21 sketch albums, 23 albums and 2 portfolios of rubbings, 3 albums of certificates of merit, along with various painting reproductions. His vigorous enthusiasm in creating works and promoting the metal world is shown in the following article;

"Unlike other artists who loathed honorary posts, he accepts any official posts, and exhibited works in any exhibition if he has enough time, and because he is already so renowned, you can see that this is not for vanity. It is because he truly feels so for the benefit of the younger metal craftsmen." (*Unno Shomin-o Shoga Kotto Zasshi* 24, May 1910)

The contents of the sketch albums and scrolls are as follows; (the number of the illustrations in this book are shown on page 150)

Sketch album 1   32.0 × 40.5   (vases and figures)
Sketch album 2   32.0 × 40.5   (birds)
Sketch album 3   22.8 × 31.5   (fish and insects)
Sketch album 4   27.2 × 19.3   (incense burners, cigarette cases, dishes, etc.)

Materials related with UNNO Shomin

UNNO Shomin is one of the major modern Japanese metal carving artists, and the only metal carving professor that taught from the beginning of the Tokyo Fine Arts School throughout the Meiji era. His eldest son Toyotaro (Minjo), third son Ginzaburo (Seijo), and fourth son Kiyoshi (Shumin) all studied metal carving art at the Tokyo Fine Arts School, and Kiyoshi served as a professor at this School and continued after the School became the Tokyo National University of Fine Arts and Music in 1949. Due to this deep relationship with this University, the draft sketches, rubbings, etc. of the Unno family were donated to our University in 1970, and was titled as 'Unno Family Materials'. It is a collection of not only material of the works of the Unno Family, but it also includes designs and rubbings of other Edo to Meiji period metal craftsmen and painters. In this publication, we have selected the essence of the material related to UNNO Shomin for the illustrations, and in this essay I will introduce some sketches among them that are little known, but before that, I would like to mention briefly about UNNO Shomin himself.

Personal History of UNNO Shomin

UNNO Shomin was born on May 15th, 1814 as the fourth son of UNNO Den'emon of Mito (presently in Ibaraki Prefecture). His name as a youth was Takejiro. After studying metal carving of sword fittings under his uncle, UNNO Yoshimori I for 4 years since age 9, he then studied various metal techniques under HAGIYA Katsuhira for 11 years since age 13. He studied classical Chinese under TAKE Shojiro, and painting under ADACHI Baiken. He also studied metal hammering techniques under MYOCHIN Ki-no Yoshiomi. From a young age, he showed remarkable talent in *Tokiwazu* (*joruri* or dramatic chant accompanied by a samisen lute), traditional dance and playing samisen, and these talents played an important part in his extraordinary expression in his later works depicting traditional dancers.

Around 1867, he started his practice as a metal carving craftsmen at age 24 in Mito, and used the name Motohira receiving the latter character of his teacher Katsuhira. Around 1871, he moves to Tokyo, staying at the home of his elder brother SANADA Kojiro (Shizukuni) who was also a metal carving artist in Tokyo, and created metal fittings for bags and pouches. From around this time, he began to use the name Shomin, using Katshuhira's first character "katsu" (also can be read "sho"), and the last character of YOKOYA Somin, the great metal carving craftsman of the Edo period. In 1873, he studied carving techniques of flowers and birds under KARIKANE Morichika, and improved his skills in furnishings and personal effects such as vases and cigarette cases. He started his own business in Tokyo in 1876, the same year as the Haitō edict (stating that only those in formal uniform, military officers, and policemen were allowed to wear a sword), and had to create vases, incense burners and boxes, cigarette and cigar cases, rings and other personal accessories, instead of sword fittings.

Using the same techniques as in sword fittings, he created a metal pouch fastener in the shape of an ancient person, which received a prize at the First National Industrial Exposition in 1877. He used the name Tokasai Shomin at this time. He created the 'Sparrow and ear of rice panel', again winning a prize in the Second National Industrial Exposition in 1881. Its photograph (fig.1) shows quite higher relief than what was usually used in sword fittings. Around 1887, he created a silver breast ornament (clasp) according to the design by KANO Hogai (fig.3), on the request of William Sturgis BIGELOW, and his skill receives recognition by Ernest FENOLLOSA and OKAKURA Tenshin. Since the spring of 1887, he receives detailed guidance on the movements and costume of Raryo-o, a traditional court dance, and begins to work on a three dimensional figure of a dancer performing this. In 1890 he exhibited this work at the Third National Industrial Exposition, and received first prize of technical excellence, and the piece was purchased by the Imperial Household (now in the Museum of Imperial Collections, Sannomaru Shozokan). The same year he was employed by the Tokyo Fine Arts School, and together with KANO Natsuo, they created and put into practice the first basics of metal carving techniques within school education. In 1891, he became Associate Professor at the School. In 1893, he once again creates a piece depicting a traditional court dancer, Genjoraku, in the form of a panel receiving a bronze medal at the World's Columbian Exposition in Chicago (now in the Tokyo National Museum, sketch illustrated on p.72). He becomes Professor of the

Foreword

UNNO Shomin (1844–1915) is one of the major metal carving artists of the Meiji era, and was the professor of the Tokyo Fine Arts School (the predecessor of the Tokyo National University of Fine Arts and Music) from its initiation until the beginning of the 20th century, and rendered remarkable services to metal art education.

Since age 9, he studied metal carving under the Mito sword fitting artists UNNO Yoshimori I and HAGIYA Katsuhira, after which he started business in Tokyo, but due to the Haito edict in 1976, he was forced to give up creating sword fittings. Along with the other metal carving artists, he shifted his work to create objects fit for the new era's needs, such as vases, figures, tobacco cases, and personal accessories. He entered his works in exhibitions, such as his most famous work 'Raryo-o", and became renowned. In 1890, he became disciple of KANO Natsuo, the first metal carving professor at the Tokyo Fine Arts School, and together they created the foundations of the metal education at the School. In 1894 he became an Imperial Court Artist, and leaded the metal art world. He was especially strong in metal inlay using various colored metals fostered by his sword fitting techniques.

A vast collection of various sketches, designs and rubbings of metal work from sword fittings to vases, etc. was donated to the Tokyo National University of Fine Arts, by UNNO Shomin's grandson in 1970, and is now in the University Art Museum. These are research materials for not only the Unno family's existing works, but also include materials related to other metal works of the same era. It is quite meaningful that these are published as a part of the usage and research of the Museum collection. We hope that it will contribute to related studies, and express our deep gratitude to those who offered their generous cooperation.

The University Art Museum
Tokyo National University of Fine Arts and Music

SKETCHES OF UNNO SHOMIN
—WITHIN THE COLLECTION OF THE UNIVERSITY ART MUSEUM, TOKYO NATIONAL UNIVERSITY OF FINE ARTS AND MUSIC